Jim Gardner
A Question of Character

by

Grady Jefferys
and
Charles Heatherly

The Patriot Press
Raleigh, NC

Contents

Jim Gardner...Unique In This Century 11

Champ to Chump 16

The Question of Character 26

The Hardees Story 39

Politics: A Fire In His Belly 47

In Congress But Seldom There 58

1968-1972: Twice Up, Twice Down 68

Family Inns of America:
Gardner's Business Empire Begins to Crumble 82

Other Business Ventures Go Belly Up 88

1988, New Version of Old Gardner 100

Gardner In The Crystal Ball:
What Kind of Governor Would He Be? 107

Unanswered Questions 117

Bibliography 124

Copyright, 1992
The Patriot Press
P. O. Box 1992
Raleigh, North Carolina 27602
All rights reserved
Library of Congress Catalog Card Number Pending
Distributed through arrangements with Down Home Press
Asheboro, North Carolina
First Edition, August, 1992
Printed In the United States of America

A Question of Character

... Jim Gardner, The Businessman

Jim Gardner is North Carolina's only candidate for Governor whose string of business failures left hundreds of investors, vendors and suppliers with huge financial losses. Gardner walked away from those businesses, pointing the finger of blame at other people and "circumstances." He never repaid the millions of dollars lost in those ventures and he has never accepted personal responsibility for those failures.

* * * * *

Wilber Hardee, the man whose name adorns the signs on some 3,600 Hardee's Restaurants, adamantly denies that Gardner had anything to do with building the first Hardee's Restaurant.

"If Jim Gardner says he founded Hardee's, he is lying," said Hardee. "I founded Hardee's. Jim Gardner and Leonard Rawls came along and tricked me out of my store and my name."

... Jim Gardner, Private Citizen

"Wesleyan College is the best example of civic pride in Rocky Mount," says a former trustee of the school. "It is the one thing that cuts across religion, politics and everything. Everybody who is anybody is asked to do something, at some time, for Wesleyan, and Jim Gardner has never done anything. If you find somebody in Rocky Mount who doesn't do something for Wesleyan, you'll find he doesn't do anything for anyone."

* * * * *

Gardner is the only candidate for Governor of either party ever to come before the electorate owning no stake in the state he wishes to head. His Nash County property statements show that he is without any material possession--not a home, not a car, not a chair. In 1991, he paid not one penny in property taxes in the county in which he lives.

... Jim Gardner, The Politician

Gardner's 1992 campaign for Governor is his sixth campaign for public office in North Carolina.

* * * * *

Gardner, recognizing that he was a better debater than the aging Harold Cooley, constantly baited Cooley to debate him on television during his campaign for Congress in 1966. When a joint appearance at N.C. State University was filmed by two television stations, Gardner had his media consultant purchase the film and edit the raw footage into what appeared to be a debate between the two candidates. Gardner's campaign then purchased time to broadcast the doctored film.

* * * * *

When he was appointed to the House Committee on Education and Labor, Congressman Jim Gardner was so proud that he sent out a special news release announcing the appointment. However, Gardner did not attend a single meeting of the House Education and Labor Committee during the entire year of 1968. Nor did he attend any of its subcommittee meetings.

* * * * *

In his 1968 campaign for Governor, Gardner solicited funds by telling contributors that everyone who contributed $1,000 to his campaign would have special, coded stationery for communicating with the Governor's office. He promised these contributors preferred treatment. Publicity from the incident was so embarrassing to Gardner's campaign that Gardner issued a press release blaming the incident on a staff member.

* * * * *

... Jim Gardner, The Lieutenant Governor

One of the ideas advanced by Lieutenant Governor Jim Gardner and the North Carolina Drug Cabinet, which he headed, was a "Marijuana Watch Program," in which citizens would keep an eye out for marijuana plants set by drug dealers.

After 18 months, Gardner called a news conference to announce the fruits of the project and displayed 22 marijuana plants which a state employee had found growing on the right-of-way of I-95 near Benson, possibly the result of seeds blown from a passing car.

After 18 months and an expenditure of nearly $123,000, this was all Gardner was able to produce for his "Marijuana Watch Program," at a cost to taxpayers of $5,590 per plant.

Acknowledgements

A book about a major political candidate for high public office requires the assistance of many people. During the course of gathering material for this book, we have talked with dozens, perhaps hundreds, of men and women of both political parties who have provided information and insight about Jim Gardner, the various campaigns in which he has participated, and the business ventures in which he has been involved over the years.

We express our appreciation to all who shared their recollections and their insights, and who helped in the search for information and perspective.

Special appreciation is extended to Wilber Hardee of Greenville, North Carolina, the founder of Hardee's Restaurants who has never received the credit he deserves for his pioneering vision.

We are also indebted to Jack Hawke, Chairman of the Republican Party of North Carolina; Mayo Boddie, Chairman of Boddie-Noell Enterprises; C. C. Cameron, former State Budget Director and former Chief Executive Officer and Chairman of the Board of First Union National Bank and a founding partner of Cameron-Brown; Peter Ploss, a former associate of Jim Gardner in the Carolando Center Development; Nash County Sheriff Frank Brown; Sal Montalbano, who spoke candidly about his ongoing litigation with Gardner at the time of this writing; Bob Burtman, of the Durham Independent; curator of the North Carolina Collection at the University of North Carolina at Chapel Hill; the Wake County Library system for its excellent file of newspaper clippings which supported the recollections of many people; and the Durham Herald-Sun for permission to use the cover photo by staff photographer Bernard Thomas.

Dedicated to the people of North Carolina.

"Characters do not change. Opinions alter, but characters are only developed."

Benjamin Disraeli

Foreword

In recent times, candidates for public office, their supporters, news reporters and voters, seriously interested in the issues of the day and concerns about the future, have all complained about news coverage of politics and politicians.

The television soundbite--that snippet of video footage containing the voice of a candidate often uttering something provocative, frequently something silly and rarely anything profound--has been singled out for special criticism. Those little bites have been shrinking in recent years until the average TV soundbite is only 10 seconds in length, hardly long enough to explain the issues of our times.

The 30-second TV commercial, favored by candidates, is not a better vehicle for an intelligent discussion of significant issues or the background, experience and wisdom of those seeking public office.

Newspapers, which as recently as 20 years ago provided the major source of information about politicians and political campaigns, have lost circulation in the "video age," and many have reduced their emphasis on comprehensive coverage of candidates and campaigns.

Concurrently, thoughtful voters have expressed an interest in new and different methods of acquiring information about politics.

The developing trends in the media, combined with changing public attitudes, seemed to present an opportunity to the authors to fill a need. We concluded that by publishing books about candidates for high public office, we would tap the discontent of the public, provide in-depth coverage of candidates and campaigns, and, thus, do well by doing good.

Initially, we considered doing books on gubernatorial candidates from both the Democratic and Republican Parties. Confronted with the daunting task of gathering information, writing, editing, printing and distributing books, we were forced to scale back the scope of our venture.

As we were pondering the decision, the Democratic candidate preempted our efforts by announcing that he would issue a series of exhaustive position papers, thoroughly explaining his *position on numerous issues. Thus, we decided on the Republican candidate, Jim Gardner, as the subject for our first book.*

Several factors about the life of Gardner make him a worthy subject. He had been out of public life for a long time prior to winning North Carolina's Lieutenant Governor's office in 1988. His public and private lives were filled with peaks and valleys. Controversy frequently has followed in his wake.

We hoped--and genuinely expected--that Gardner would welcome our efforts, that he would grant us a series of interviews from which we could gain insight and perspective about his past, his present and his future goals for North Carolina.

Gardner did not welcome our attention. Instead, he seemed determined from the outset to disclose nothing to us that would aid us in our journalistic efforts.

Writing a book about Gardner became a challenge. What did he have to hide? Why did he shun us during a time when politicians seek attention? We began the research for this book with these paramount questions.

Our systematic search led us to court records, to an astonishingly long trail of acrimonious legal charges and litigation, a grand jury indictment, foreclosures on businesses, judgments for unpaid bills and congressional hearings.

During interviews with loyal Republicans, we discovered a pattern. No one praised the accomplishments of Gardner. No one lauded either his vision or commitment to high standards of performance. Instead, even his staunchest supporters were defensive about Gardner, his record in business and his record in public service.

After several months of interviewing people familiar with Gardner's business and public life, and after reviewing the numerous public records dealing with various aspects of his life, we came to the conclusion that profound questions hang over the head of Jim Gardner as he comes before North Carolina voters in 1992, asking for their trust. In our judgment, these questions go to the very core of his character.

Our book presents the issues which raise the questions of Gardner's character. It does not, however, answer all of those questions. This, we leave to you.

The Image
As Conveyed By A Radio Commercial:

Gardner Radio Ad
Summer 1992

Thirty years ago, before the grandchildren and the gray hair, he was a struggling young businessman from Rocky Mount with a wonderful wife and three children.
He worked long, and hard, and late.
And by his early thirties, he had started Hardee's, one of the world's most successful fast food chains, and launched other bold new businesses, until the gas crunch, high interest rates and the recession in the early 70s took nearly everything he owned.
He started over, building up a new restaurant business-- working in the kitchen--for ten years, until he came back.
Today the hair is silver, and Jim Gardner is a grandfather. Our conservative Lieutenant Governor.
And unlike professional politicians who have never worked for a living, Jim Gardner understands us.
Real experience protecting us.
Jim Gardner, Governor.

The Reality

Behind his carefully crafted media messages is an entirely different Jim Gardner. In its comprehensive review of his life and times, this book examines the contradictions between the Gardner image and the Gardner reality.

Jim Gardner
Unique In This Century

Since the turn of the century, more than a hundred North Carolinians have offered themselves as candidates for the office of Governor of North Carolina. All were different, of course. However, the great majority of the candidates of the past 90 years have shared something in common. They have come before the public with distinguished records of service, often in many fields of endeavor. Jim Gardner brings no such record to the campaign for Governor of North Carolina. Instead, he brings a business record that would cast doubt on the qualifications of anyone seeking any position of responsibility. His political record consists of one term as a U. S. Congressman, during which he abrogated his responsibilities to run for Governor, and one term as Lieutenant Governor during which his responsibilities have been essentially ceremonial. In three out of five attempts to gain public office, Gardner has been repudiated by North Carolina voters.

Gardner's explanation of his business and political failings simply withers under careful scrutiny, thus calling into question the character of this man who would be governor.

Gardner is North Carolina's first candidate of the 20th century of any party to come before the electorate dragging behind him the corpses of numerous failed enterprises. The stench of pervasive business failure clings to him despite his best efforts to obscure his own role in those failures. His inability to manage his own business mocks his promises to operate government on a "business-like" basis.

Gardner is the only candidate for Governor in the history of North Carolina who has been indicted for securities violations. Although he was not tried on the charge as result of a jurisdictional ruling by the court, the indictment, and the way it was handled called into question his professed commitment to law and order.

Gardner is North Carolina's only candidate for Governor who has been successfully sued for what was essentially the theft of advertising materials. While he was still associated with Hardee's, Gardner engaged a firm to produce an advertising jingle. As was customary, the company produced a demonstration tape for review. Gardner required his advertising agency to use the demonstration tape in a large-scale advertising program without paying for its usage. His own advertising agent, Gene Lewis of Rocky Mount, North Carolina, testified that he had urged Gardner not to use the demonstration tape without paying for it.

Gardner is the only candidate for Governor of either party to come before the electorate apparently owning no stake in the State he wishes to head. His property tax statements in his home county show that he is without any material possessions--not a home, not a car, not even a chair. Today, he and his wife live on the estate of his deceased father-in-law, and in 1991 he paid not one penny in property taxes in the county in which he lives.

If elected, Gardner would be the only Governor of North Carolina in the 20th Century who would not have a college degree, a license to practice law or a record of personal scholarship in any field.

In 1968, a thin paperback volume entitled <u>Jim Gardner, A</u>

Time To Speak was issued with his byline. Subsequently, it was learned that the book was mostly written by David Wilson, a political operative for Gardner who later sued him for mismanagement of a company in which Wilson was a investor.

Gardner is North Carolina's only candidate for Governor whose string of business failures left dozens of investors and hundreds of vendors and suppliers with huge financial losses. Gardner walked away from those businesses, pointing fingers of blame at other people and "circumstances." He never repaid the millions of dollars lost in those ventures and he has never accepted personal responsibility for the failures. In spite of well-documented evidence to the contrary, his supporters say that Gardner has repaid his debts.

Gardner is North Carolina's only candidate for Governor to come before the electorate with a history of dozens of unsatisfied legal judgments lodged against him by people who are convinced he is a deadbeat.

Gardner is North Carolina's only candidate for Governor who has taken steps to organize his finances and assets so as to prevent their being seized for debts he might have incurred.

A Durham newspaper, The Independent, reported in the spring of 1992 that Gardner and his businesses have defaulted on at least $34 million in loans. Gardner's failed businesses, reported The Independent, have stuck more than 450 suppliers and employees for at least $2.7 million in unpaid bills and wages. Gardner has repeatedly refused to comment on the newspaper accounts with the authors of this book. More than 60 lawsuits have been filed against Gardner and his companies for a variety of reasons, including failure to pay debts and breach of contract.

Other businessmen have suffered reversals of fortune. The famous Hunt brothers, heirs to a massive fortune in oil and dozens of other businesses, managed to fritter away much of their inheritance in a foolish attempt in the early 1980s to corner the market on silver.

Many of the high flyers of the boom years of the 80s--S&L, real estate, publishing, and securities moguls most notably--have made the transition from champ to chump in the realistic years of the early 1990s. None has offered himself as a candidate for office on the basis of financial acumen.

Veteran business writers for North Carolina newspapers and business journals cannot recall another political figure with such an extensive record of business failure.

Being one of North Carolina's worst businessmen of recent times could, in some circumstances, be cause for sympathy. However, Gardner precludes public sympathy for his plight by insisting that it is his business record which, more than anything else, qualifies him to lead North Carolina and manage its annual budget of $8 billion.

Gardner has laced many of his political speeches and statements with references to the need for North Carolina to operate on a businesslike basis. He has boasted of his experience in starting businesses and meeting payrolls. He contends that he has a businessman's appreciation for the need to spend money prudently and to get a dollars worth of value for every dollar spent.

Again, the Gardner record mocks the Gardner rhetoric. While his businesses were falling like dominoes in the early 1970s, Gardner drew extravagant salaries and fees from them which enabled him to hide failure behind a facade of success.

Even as he was hounded by hundreds of creditors demanding payment for millions of dollars in bad debts, Gardner lived comfortably in a stylish house in an affluent section of Rocky Mount. He drove luxury cars and his family enjoyed the use of a nice beach home on North Carolina's famous Outer Banks. How did he do it?

The answer is found partly in the will of his father-in-law, the late Arthur Lynwood Tyler, one of Eastern North Carolina's most well-respected and highly regarded business men. Tyler was frequently called by his peers, the "merchant prince" of Eastern North Carolina. He was the local partner in more than a dozen Belk-Tyler stores scattered throughout the eastern part of the state.

Tyler was a pillar in the Rocky Mount community. He was active in numerous civic causes and contributed generously to charitable events. At the peak of his civic career, he served as Chairman of the Board of Wesleyan College.

When Tyler prepared his will in 1963, he named his wife and only daughter, Marie, as his heirs. But in 1974, during Gardner's financial troubles, when foreclosures and judgments were piling up against Gardner's numerous business ventures, Tyler changed his will. He deleted Marie, Gardner's wife, from the will and stipulated that after the death of his wife, his estate go to a trust to be managed at that time by Planters National Bank which has since become Centura Bank.

At the time of his death in 1978, Tyler left an estate valued at $2.1 million, according to probate papers in the Nash County Courthouse. The estate passed first to Mrs. Tyler, and then upon her death to the trust.

The house that Gardner and his family live in now on Shady Circle in Rocky Mount and all of the property which they enjoy is owned by the trust of the late Arthur Tyler and is beyond the control of Gardner, and beyond the reach of his creditors.

Throughout his business and public life, Gardner has managed to obscure the reality of his actions with dazzling imagery. It is Gardner's name that is most closely linked to the early meteoric success of the Hardee's hamburger chain, although it was Wilber Hardee who conceived the idea, the late CPA Leonard Rawls who provided the management and fiscal leadership, and two separate franchising firms -- Spartan Food Systems, incorporated by Jerry Richardson and Charles Bradshaw, and Boddie-Noell, incorporated by W. Carleton Noell and his nephews Nick and Mayo Boddie, which thrust Hardee's Restaurants into regional prominence.

In the world of business, there is a truism: It's not what you start with, but what you end up with that counts. Measured against this maxim, Gardner's business ventures count for nothing, for he has ended up to date with nothing. His early fortune was lost, and virtually all his attempts at entrepreneurship have failed, leaving hundreds of people financially hurt and many bitter.

What does this reveal about the character of James Carson Gardner?

Emerson said, "A man's fortune is the fruit of his character." At age 59, proclaiming that his business experience qualifies him to be the chief executive of North Carolina, Gardner stands bereft of fortune, and if one is to believe Emerson, he, therefore, is bereft of character.

Surely he is unique among the hundreds of men who have offered themselves as candidates for Governor of North Carolina.

II

Champ to Chump

The Gardner business record is a byzantine trail of grandiose promises, grand beginnings and humiliating failures. It is pock-marked with pain and suffering resulting from financial losses that in some cases brought stalwart investors to their very knees and left suppliers, vendors and employees of the failed companies wringing their hands in despair.

The history of many of Gardner's business ventures is written in hundreds of pages of legal documents in which nothing less than economic atrocity is charged by friends and associates of this man who would be Governor.

More than anything else, the Gardner business record is a record of ineptitude on the part of an unschooled, ego-driven financial philistine whose grasp clearly exceeded his reach.

On the day he filed for Governor, Gardner issued a

challenge to North Carolina voters to examine his business record, which he contends is his strongest qualification for public office.

"I will put my business record on the line," Gardner said.

Following is a brief summary of the successes and failures that comprise the Gardner business record.

Hardee's

Gardner often cites his experience with Hardee's in terms designed to impress listeners with the notion that he co-founded the company and was responsible to a large extent for its early success. He often says he once headed the company.

Wilber Hardee, the man whose name adorns the 3,600 Hardee's Restaurants now in operation, tells a different story.

The first Hardee's fast food restaurant was established in Greenville, North Carolina in 1960 by Hardee. In the fall of 1960, Gardner and Rawls, an accountant, made Hardee an offer to develop a national franchise system featuring his concept and his name in return for half the ownership in his restaurant. They promised, according to Hardee, to make the company's name a household word and generate riches for each of them.

The facts show that Gardner did not co-found Hardee's. He did serve briefly as president of a corporation called Hardee's Drive-Ins. Corporation records indicate that Gardner was president of Hardee's Drive-Ins Inc. in September of 1961. Two months later an amendment to the charter was filed, changing the name of the company to Hardee's Food System, Inc., and naming J. Leonard Rawls president, a position he held until 1975. The change gave Rawls and Gardner effective voting control of the company. Hardee said that his original agreement with Gardner and Rawls provided he would hold 50 percent ownership and exercise equal control with them.

Hardee contends that, in January of 1961, Gardner and Rawls enticed him sign an agreement which gave themselves full control of Hardee's name and full benefit of all proceeds from future franchise sales. Hardee says he signed the agreement during a drinking bout with Rawls without reading the document.

Questioned by a reporter about Hardee's allegations during his 1988 campaign for Lieutenant Governor, Gardner said that he knew nothing about them.

The Hardee's franchise concept proved to be popular. By 1966 Hardees had grown to some 200 franchise stores and Gardner's stock had made him rich. After winning a seat in the U. S. Congress, Gardner resigned as vice president of the company to go to Washington, representing North Carolina's Fourth District.

In 1967, Hardee's was successfully sued in Federal Court in Wilson for using without authority or payment a jingle created by Phil Davis Musical Enterprises of New York. Although Gardner denied responsibility, other Hardee's officials testified under oath that Gardner made the decision to use the jingle without paying for it.

The jury found that Hardee's had infringed on Davis' copyright and the court ordered Hardee's to pay Davis $16,750 and make no further use of the jingle.

In 1976, Hardee's sued Gardner and obtained a judgment against him in the amount of $271,000 which he eventually paid. Details of the legal action are missing from the file in the Nash County Courthouse.

Family Inns of America

In 1971, Gardner formed Family Inns of America (FIA) to build and operate economy motels at busy interchanges on interstate highways in the Carolinas. Six motels, including three owned by Gardner, were built during the next two years. Many North Carolinians were persuaded to invest millions of dollars which they lost in 1973 when the company defaulted on its obligations. Banks and lending institutions foreclosed on the company's assets and forced Gardner out. Gardner said he, too, lost heavily.

In 1974, Gardner was sued by longtime friend and associate David Wilson over FIA stock he bought for $67,000 which became worthless. In his complaint, Wilson accused Gardner of mismanagement, negligence and fraud. The suit was settled out of court.

In 1976, Gardner was indicted for securities fraud in connection with his plan to sell FIA stock. The case was dismissed in Superior Court in Wilmington on the unusual grounds that the court did not have jurisdiction. Jurisdictional issues are rarely settled at the Superior Court level but most often at the appellate level. Gardner's attorney, the late Charles Winberry of Rocky Mount, manipulated the timing of the case in order to get it tried before an old friend on the bench.

The following year Winberry sued Gardner and won a judgment in the amount of $11,121.54 for nonpayment of legal fees arising from the FIA indictment. The judgment remained unpaid for more than a decade. Gardner made no attempt to settle the debt until 1988, as he was gearing up his campaign for Lieutenant Governor. Gardner gave the law firm a promissory note and one payment was made. No additional payments had been made between then and the spring of 1992.

While refusing to answer questions about this chapter in his business career, Gardner's campaign staff issued its version of the Family Inns debacle. As his campaign for Governor got underway, the chairman of Gardner's campaign organization issued a memo providing a carefully scripted response to criticism regarding the failure of Family Inns of America.

"When they tell you: Jim Gardner started a chain of budget motels that lost money. You tell them the truth: Yes, Family Inns of America did fail to reach its full potential. Jim Gardner personally lost well over a million dollars when the gas crisis of 1974 brought interstate travel to a stand still, leaving the highways empty of the traffic necessary to make Family Inns a success. Even though the timing was bad due to circumstances he couldn't control, his vision was once again correct as we see today how well budget motels are doing."

The memo fails to mention that, according to court records, Gardner's Family Inns of America was in deep financial trouble beginning in the middle of 1973, well before either the energy crisis or the advent of high interest rates.

And, the prepared campaign response makes no mention of other troubling facts about the company's affairs.

Modular Corporation of America

In 1971, Gardner was a principal in the forming Modular Corporation of America (MCA), to produce modular units for Family Inns of America. Although Gardner said he was not actively involved in the operation of the company, bankruptcy records show that in 1973 he received a salary of $52,500 and was the company's highest paid official.

During the company's financial troubles, Gardner and a partner, Hal Wenal, sold Modular Corporation to three convicted felons who wiped out the company's bank accounts before the company was taken back. While Gardner says today that he has never been bankrupt, his "fingerprints" are all over the MCA petition for bankruptcy protection in early 1974. When the company was liquidated, hundreds of suppliers and vendors were left with unpaid bills totalling $1.6 million.

Among the big losers in the MCA bankruptcy were the IRS and the North Carolina Department of Revenue for a total of more than $150,000. It was in May of 1973 that Gardner received his $52,500 salary and bonus from MCA. That was also the month the company stopped paying its taxes. Yet two months later, in July of 1973, executives of the company bought themselves an airplane for $60,000.

During bankruptcy proceedings Gardner was forced to pay back some $20,000 which he had "borrowed" during the company's final, troubled hours.

Although Gardner won't talk about the specifics of his business record, his campaign staff has prepared a defense for the questions which voters might have. In a memo dated May 14, 1992, the campaign chairman admonished Gardner supporters, "When you hear or read of an attack on Jim Gardner's character, take a stand and give the facts. When they tell you: Jim Gardner went bankrupt, You tell them the truth: Neither Jim Gardner nor any business controlled by him ever declared bankruptcy."

That suggested response splits hairs exceedingly fine. While Gardner was only the vice president of Modular Corporation at the time of its bankruptcy petition in 1974, he exerted substantial influence over the company's day-to-day operations.

Carolando

In 1972, Jim Gardner announced a major resort complex in Orlando, Florida, near the entrance to Disney World. Called Carolando Center, it was presented as the largest motor inn and convention center in the world. On the strength of these projections and Gardner's salesmanship, Cameron Brown Investment Group (CBIG) arranged $20 million in construction loans. A year later the company was $2 million in the red, Jim Gardner was forced out of the company and it was dissolved. First Union National Bank, CBIG's parent, took over the ailing development and found a buyer in a desperate effort to recover its principal. Individual investors lost more than $1.5 million.

Peter Ploss, an associate of Gardner's at Carolando, described Gardner as a "snake-oil salesman." He said Gardner is "perhaps the world's greatest salesman but worst manager."

Brandywine Bay

Brandywine Bay is an upscale, 1,100-acre golf resort in Morehead City, North Carolina, begun by Gardner in 1972, about the same time as Carolando Center, with $9 million borrowed through CBIG. By 1975 Brandywine Bay was deep in debt to vendors, suppliers and employees. Suppliers owed more than $1 million were never paid. Gardner was forced out when CBIG foreclosed on the property and eventually found a buyer who completed the development.

Today, Gardner passes off the failure of these businesses as the result of the energy crisis and high interest rates. However, these failures all occurred during the Republican administration of Richard Nixon, well before the Arab oil embargo and before the era of escalating interest rates.

Virginia Waffle Shoppes

In 1972, Gardner formed Virginia Waffle Shoppes to operate primarily in North Carolina. A Small Business Administration loan, in the amount of $200,000, was approved for the first franchise through the Richmond, Virginia SBA office. However, before the SBA loan was funded, Gardner's partner in the venture was indicted for fraud and a scandal erupted in the top ranks of the Richmond SBA office. Testimony before the Banking Committee of the U. S. House of Representatives the following year indicated that Gardner's partner in the Virginia Waffle Shoppes had ties to organized crime and that Gardner had submitted the SBA loan application as a minority entrepreneur.

Federal auditors found a number of irregularities with the

transaction. A SBA official testified that the government would have lost $100,000 had the loan been processed.

Parker's Barbecue

In 1982, Gardner was sued by Parker's Barbecue of Wilson for breach of contract and for attempting to misappropriate the good name of Parker's Barbecue, one of the best known purveyors of barbecue in North Carolina. Gardner had been operating Parker's Barbecue franchises in Rocky Mount for nearly a decade under an agreement signed in 1971. When Gardner stopped making the franchise payments in 1981 and put up a billboard in Rocky Mount implying that Parker's Barbecue had closed and had been taken over by Gardner, the Parkers sued. The case was settled out of court in 1983.

Gardner's Barbecue

In the early 1980s, Gardner and his brother, John G. Gardner, established Gardner Foods, Inc., which exists today, but not at the level Gardner predicted.

During an expansion into Raleigh in 1984, Gardner predicted that 10 Gardner's Barbecue restaurants, a spinoff from Gardner Foods, would be operating in Raleigh within two years. Six opened in Raleigh but only one remains in business today. At the peak of Gardner's Barbecue success 16 restaurants existed, but by 1992, that number had shrunk to seven restaurants.

During the 80s, Gardner Foods opened several restaurants under the name of Friday's 1890 Seafood Restaurants but was forced, in court, to change the name by TGI Friday's. The restaurants were renamed Fosdick's and all closed or were sold.

Although Gardner mentioned the barbecue restaurants as proof of his business comeback in television ads during his 1988 campaign for Lieutenant Governor, there is a question regarding ownership. While he claims to have played a major role in the Gardner's Barbecue Restaurants, he does not list any property from these facilities on his Nash County tax listing.

While Gardner was building and operating his restaurant facilities during the mid 80s he was telling the Sheriff of Nash County, Frank Brown, that he had no assets which could be seized to pay off judgments totalling millions resulting from his business failures and unpaid debts during the previous decade.

Sheriff Brown recalls that at one time he had " a bushel full of judgments" against Gardner and was pressed by lawyers from around the country to explain why he couldn't collect.

Current Case

In the summer of 1992, Gardner faced a suit brought by Sal Montalbano and his wife, Peggy. The Montalbanos charged Gardner with breach of contract in the subleasing of a building originally leased by Gardner for a barbecue restaurant.

The Montalbanos contend that while they were making renovations and installing new equipment to the building, Gardner failed to make lease payments, as he had agreed to do, causing them to be evicted from the building and to lose the equipment they had installed.

The property in question is located on Gorman Street, near N.C. State University in Raleigh. Montalbano contends he lost $78,900 because of Gardner's breach of contract. Montalbano was repaying the loan at $575 per month in the summer of 1992.

The loss has caused Montalbano great emotional stress. He suffered a mental breakdown in the spring of 1992 during which he threatened to kill himself.

"I want my money back," Montalbano said. "I need it."

Montalbano, a former political supporter of Gardner, worked as a volunteer in Gardner's 1972 campaign for Governor. "That is why I trusted the man," Montalbano said. "I told my wife that this man once ran for Governor. Surely we can trust him."

Has his opinion of Gardner changed?

"Jim Gardner is an unethical man," Montalbano said. "He beat me out of all the money I had in the world. No I wouldn't trust him again. I won't vote for him either."

Nonpayment of Wages

In 1988, Gardner was sued, in the middle of his campaign for Lieutenant Governor, by two former Fosdick's employees for nonpayment of back wages. When the court refused to delay the trial, Gardner agreed to pay nearly $17,000 to the plaintiffs and their attorney as well as court costs.

A Different View
Of The Gardner Business Record

Mayo Boddie, his brother and his uncle are the principals in Boddie-Noell Enterprises, Inc., one of the two largest franchise holders of Hardee's Restaurants. The company operates more than 500 restaurants and along with Spartan Foods of Spartanburg, South Carolina, was one of the catalysts in the success of Hardee's franchise operations.

In June of 1992, Boddie, the chairman of the board of Boddie-Noell Enterprises and its chief operating officer, signed a letter praising Gardner's business record which was the centerpiece of a full-page advertisement published in major North Carolina newspapers on behalf of Gardner's gubernatorial candidacy.

In his letter, Boddie said that Gardner had been involved in successful businesses other than Hardee's.

Following publication of the advertisement, Boddie was asked to specify Gardner's other successful business ventures.

"With reference to his other business ventures," replied Boddie, "I have certainly heard of them, but I honestly do not have any insight."

Boddie recalled that he, his brother and uncle joined the Hardee's enterprise "in the very early stages." At the time, he said, "Only two Hardee's were operating."

Boddie said he and his family agreed to buy four Hardee's Restaurants at $1,500 each. "Our agreement with Jimmy (Gardner) and Leonard Rawls was a verbal one, and we had not made a deposit," recalls Boddie.

"Before a formal contract could be written and before we had given them any money, they approached us and said that another party had agreed to buy 15 franchises, but only if they could have the cities we requested."

Gardner and Rawls asked the Boddie Family to consider other locations and let them sell the franchise locations they had agreed to sell Boddie to the other buyer.

"We told them definitely not," said Boddie, ". . . that we expected them to live up to our verbal agreement. This they agreed to do."

Boddie said that while Gardner was involved with Hardee's his relationship with Gardner was "always satisfactory." Boddie said that his Hardee's Restaurants on interstate highways suffered during the period in which Gardner's Family Inns of America folded. Hardee's locations in towns and cities "helped carry the poor highway locations," Boddie said.

Another large Hardee's franchise owner, Jack C. D. Bailey, was quoted in a newspaper article in 1988 praising Gardner's "vision and work ethic."

"There isn't any question in my mind that Hardee's Food Systems would not have gotten off the ground if it had not been for Jim Gardner's enthusiasm and his vision and his willingness to work around the clock to make it happen." Bailey was quoted as saying in an article in the Raleigh News and Observer.

Although Gardner's business record is replete with legal actions, foreclosures, dozens of judgments for unpaid bills and wages, and a criminal indictment, Gardner still commands the loyalty of some business people. Many of them have profited from the Hardee's success. Others seem to be unaware of or unable to accept the reality of Gardner's extensive business failures.

III

The Question of Character

Gardner's acquaintances say he is an affable companion for an idle afternoon of boating, fishing, tennis or some other sport. By all indications, he is a devoted husband and father, genuinely interested in family life, and his record indicates that he has a will -- perhaps even a compulsion -- to excel in some public endeavor.

As a candidate for public office which carries the burden of public trust, Gardner's character is called into question on the basis of his activities in three areas:

1. Business: He sold other people on the merits of his grandiose business ideas, persuaded them to invest in his schemes, and when the business failed, often because of his bad timing, lack of management skills, negligence or worse, sought to evade responsibility for the consequences. Subsequent chapters will provide ample details of the damage done to others, of Gardner's

unwillingness to assume financial responsibility and of a lifelong pattern he has followed to insulate and protect himself from legitimate creditors who seek to collect the debts he incurs.

2. Personal Honesty: Gardner seems to believe, perhaps sincerely, that "perception is reality." He has been caught by no less than former Governor Jim Holshouser and Presidential aide Harry Dent -- both fellow Republicans -- in outright fabrication. His statements regarding his business activities and his business failures seem to be structured not to disclose, but to deceive. He seems to be capable of declaring that black is white, that day is night, that right is wrong and wrong is right, oblivious to the fact that the contrary is evident to everyone. Ah, but don't all politicians lie? Perhaps some do, but few politicians do it with the degree of self-righteous arrogance that characterizes the Gardner statements which have been disproved by time and events.

3. Performance in Public Office: Gardner's record as a U.S. Congressman can be described precisely by only one word -- shameful. His attendance record was one of the worst in the history of the U. S. Congress. His record of service was non-existent. His term of office was replete with publicity-seeking and political posturing. His correspondence with constituents reflects muddled thinking on issues of vital concern. A generation later, as North Carolina's first Republican Lieutenant Governor of the 20th Century, Gardner proved that time had taught him very little. He can point to not one achievement of value to North Carolina governance that bears his signature or his fingerprints. His opportunity to serve a genuine need -- as chairman of the Drug Cabinet -- is stained by political payoffs to cronies and contributors and the waste of millions of dollars in tax money. As he was as a U. S. Congressman, Gardner, as Lieutenant Governor, has been a politically posturing publicity seeker and a campaigner for higher office.

In the human spirit and the human heart, redemption is always a possibility, but for Gardner, now approaching the sunset of his life, excellence in governance seems further and further from his reach.

To answer the many questions concerning the Gardner character, it is essential to look backward--to the shifting winds of fate that bent the twig into the tree and the slings and arrows of the mischievous fortune that shaped this man who would be governor.

Much is known about the life and times of Jim Gardner, the candidate, who before redeeming himself politically in 1988, was in danger of becoming known as the Harold Stassen of the Tar Heel State. Like fellow Republican Stassen, Gardner was elected to Congress early in life, lost his seat and then ran in many failed campaigns over the decades.

Much is known about Gardner, the Congressman, who after a slash-and-burn campaign against the veteran Harold Cooley, discovered that he did not like Congress, and like a petulant child forced to do an unpleasant task, refused to participate.

Much is known about Gardner the failed businessman who left so much financial carnage in his wake that many of his associates today are extremely leery of his business proposals.

Much is known about Gardner, the Phoenix-like figure who has risen from the ashes of the fires of failure which once consumed him.

Indeed, the many facades of Jim Gardner are familiar, but few, if any, truly know this man who has the awesome audacity to present himself in public forums on the premise that a lifetime of failure qualifies him for the State's highest office.

Many might wonder if Jim Gardner is moved by some inner, inexplicable compulsion to expose himself and his scabbed over sores?

The record of failure which Gardner waves as a banner of success, the ease with which he appropriates unto himself the creative output of others bespeak intellectual vacuity run amuck, fueled perhaps by megalomania.

Character, says Webster's Unabridged Dictionary, is the sum total of all of the parts of a human being. To many, character is simply "moral excellence," the willingness to do the right thing when the right thing might not be easy, expedient, profitable or pleasant.

In a definitive study of presidential character, Dr. James David Barber, Chairman of the Duke University Department of Political Science, set forth ways to predict the future performance of presidents, based on an understanding of their character, their world view and their style. His formula serves as well for governors.

"Character," writes Dr. Barber, "is the person's stance as he confronts experience. It is formed early in life. The best way to predict character, is to see how it was put together in the first place."

Jim Gardner is the oldest of three sons born in 1933, in the depths of economic depression, to Mr. and Mrs. James Cuthrell Gardner. Although Gardner was too young to personally experience hard times, he is of the right age to have grown up hearing the horror stories of "the Great Depression."

Many people suffered during those times, to be sure, and by the time Gardner was old enough for the stories to have genuine impact, they had been embellished for maximum dramatic impact. Hardly a person alive of Gardner's generation could avoid having his perception of life shaped by the stories of hardship and deprivation that were rooted in the reality of the depression.

For many, the stories instilled fear of an environment over which one had little or no control. Children of depression-era parents and grandparents grew up with the certainty that no matter how good things might be at present, they could be lost in an uncertain future. Gardner's experience in the real world of business fulfilled the prophecy of those who had suffered similar fates in another time.

Not much is known of the hopes and fears and dreams that shaped the boy into the man he was to become. Although born during the depression, Gardner grew up in middle class affluence. He seems to have enjoyed a rather placid childhood and adolescent. The highs and lows that give life drama seem to have been absent in Gardner's early years. One thing that is known about Gardner is his ability to sell. Indeed, a large component of the Gardner personality and character is salesmanship. A good salesman is essential to the success of a product or an idea, and Gardner has earned the respect of friend and foe for his ability to persuade people to purchase his products, whether they be hamburger franchise or political notions.

Where did he get that ability -- and why? Gardner's academic achievements and his approach to serious pursuits would indicate that early in his formative years, he discovered that he could substitute salesmanship for substantive intellectual effort and physical output.

"To people who did not know him", says a Raleigh Democrat who was involved in a failed Gardner business, "the man could make you believe the sun would rise in the west and set in the east. He has a gift of gab."

Some forms of successful salesmanship derive from a careful presentation of relevant information, from anticipating questions about products or concepts and having the answers by the time the questions are asked.

Other forms of salesmanship -- the kind that damage the reputation of the selling profession -- stem from a slick and purposeful manipulation of information by the unscrupulous to exploit the unwary.

From his public statements regarding his business plans early in life to his political rhetoric, to his attempt to offer his numerous failures in many spheres of life as a basis for dealing with the serious political issues of the 1990s, Gardner is a practiced master at manipulating information.

Millions of men and women define themselves by periods in which they reach adulthood--such as "turn of the century," "the roaring twenties," "the Depression," pre-war (meaning pre World War II), World War II, etc.

Gardner is a product of the forties and the fifties, shaped and formed, by those times, albeit perhaps unwillingly, as surely as a coastal scrub oak is shaped and twisted by the ocean wind.

As children, males of Gardner's age watched older family members and friends march off to save the world from the tyranny of the Nazis and the "Japs." The media of the time -- newspapers and radio -- glamorized the exploits of brave GIs. For youngsters of Gardner's age, the opportunity to contribute to the noble cause was restricted to collecting scrap metal, buying and saving stamps, chopping weeds in "victory" gardens, and doing without. It was hardly the stuff of which heroes were made. The fighting, the suffering, the winning that were occurring overseas -- from those crucibles emerged genuine heroes. The youngsters of Gardner's generation grew up in the shadows of those returning GIs who had travelled, faced history's most infamous tyrants and returned in triumph.

Not only were males of Gardner's generation overshadowed

by the exploits of the generation immediately ahead of them, they were overwhelmed by the numbers. During the hard times of the Great Depression the nation's birth rate was the lowest in history. When Gardner was born in 1933, the economic fortunes of the nation as well as the birth rate were at their lowest ebbs. In the 1920s, a time of booming prosperity, the birth rate had been high. In the post war period that began in 1945, the birth rate soared, producing what is commonly known as baby boomers.

Persons born in the mid 1930s who came to adulthood in the mid-fifties have been called the "silent generation." More appropriately, they are the "lonely generation." Most of their lives have been spent interacting with people a decade older or a decade younger than they. Not necessarily by choice, but by demographic imperatives.

When Gardner reached his teen years, the term "teenager" was new. Adolescents then as now were troublesome, but mostly quiet. That small number of young people between the generation that had recently returned from saving the world with stories to tell and that huge bawling, squalling mass of baby boomers would have been drowned out had it raised its voice to protest the conditions of the times.

The adolescents and young adults of the fifties were not given to challenging the status quo. For the most part they adopted and adapted. They adopted the hair styles and clothing of returning GIs, danced to the music of big bands which ever so slowly evolved into an innocent kind of rock and roll. And they adapted to the demands of older generations in business, the professions and the arts who required a kind of agreeable conformity.

Men and women of Gardner's generation grew up respectful of their elders and contemptuously envious of their more free-spirited juniors. Even Elvis Presley, the rock and roll king of the fifties, was deferential to just about everyone, lacing his speech with yessirs, nosirs and the like.

For the generation of the fifties, times were not oppressive. The older generation, recognizing that the young men who had just come of age looked up to them and wanted to please, and realizing that they were few in number, welcomed them into the establishment. They opened doors, showed them the ropes and shepherded them through the rites of passage into the world of work.

With such a send off, men of the fifties were expected to succeed. Jim Gardner was no exception. He was conditioned by circumstance of birth, family, friends and the society in which he was reared to excel -- at something.

There were other requirements of white middle class men of the fifties. They were expected to marry well, produce fine children, and be good providers for their families. A man of the fifties could be forgiven many sins, but being a poor provider was not one of them.

Indeed, white men of middle class circumstances were expected to sow some wild oats, to fool around with women whom they did not plan to marry. Society allowed them to fumble and stumble in the early years of adulthood, but eventually they were expected to "take hold," or to make something of themselves and be good providers.

The decade in which Gardner came to adulthood is referred to now -- with some nostalgia -- as a time of innocence.

Viewed against the violence and mores of today-- gun-toting youngsters in elementary school, drugs, alcohol, shootings, knifings, public pornography, out-of-wedlock children, casual sex, unmarried couples living together, out-of-the-closet homosexuality, filthy and satanic music--almost any decade would appear to be a time of innocence.

When Gardner was a high school student in Rocky Mount no one used drugs, if you didn't count some of the older folks who took various concoctions of no proven therapeutic value.

There was alcohol, of course, but very few young women consumed alcohol in any form. Beer was sold at sleazy joints and those who drank much of it were considered to be sleazy greasers.

The racial climate of the 50s and early 60s in North Carolina was decidedly tranquil. Whites and blacks were cordial to each other in their personal relationships. Despite rigid segregation, enforced by both social mores and legal statues, black and white people developed workable relationships. Whatever their private feelings, white people of "good breeding" did not deliberately insult black people.

Whites, overwhelmingly, assumed unto themselves attitudes

a position of inferiority, which was enforced by every mechanism known to society.

White people of Gardner's generation were largely oblivious to the unfairness of such a system and the frustration, pain, and suffering that such a system inflicted on large numbers of black people. Black people did not make an issue of it. Indeed, many black people, for reasons known only to themselves, accepted the system with such equanimity that both blacks and whites had come to believe it was less than evil, and that black people actually liked a system of rigid social segregation on the basis of race.

Gardner, like many of his time, simply never had reason or inclination to question the system or to challenge the status quo.

In a decade of neon-colored innocence, Gardner advanced from childhood, through adolescence and into young adulthood. Gardner won't describe his earlier academic status, but those who know him well recall that he was not scholarly in school. Neither did he display many leadership qualities. A childhood friend remembers that one of Gardner's early teachers was unimpressed with his scholastic abilities.

Some psychologists contend that persons continuously forced to interact and socialize with members of different generations can follow either of two development paths. On the one hand, some suffer profound and pervasive alienation as adults. Always, it seems, they are out of step and out of sync with those around them. Others may develop a sense of uniqueness, a feeling that they are entirely different from those around them.

Gardner, like most of his peers, had very little understanding of or appreciation for the excesses of the baby boomers. Like most of the older generations, he was aghast at the loud, undisciplined lifestyle of the multitude of baby boomers.

Early on, though, Gardner would come to appreciate the baby boomers. Their great numbers and their huge appetite for cheap hamburgers, milkshakes, and fried potatoes were the basis for the only business success he ever attained.

Although he didn't stand out particularly, Gardner was well known in his community. His father operated a regional dairy which supplied many of the dairy products used throughout Northeastern North Carolina.

A childhood pal who grew up across the street from Gardner recalls that Gardner was popular because he had ready access to ice cream and other dairy treats.

"Jim had what appeared to be an easy life, growing up in one of Rocky Mount's most affluent neighborhoods," recalls Mack Pearsall. "He and his family were nice folks. He was always good company if you just wanted to socialize. He was affable, easy going, easy to be around."

A former legislator from Edgecombe County who grew up with Gardner does not recall Gardner ever showing leadership qualities in high school. "I don't think he was a great athlete. He certainly was not the valedictorian of his graduating class. I don't know of anything that would have made him special. He certainly did not seem to have any political ambitions -- or interests."

After high school, Gardner and college life didn't mesh very well. The record is somewhat fuzzy, with some reports indicating Gardner, because of poor grades, was forced out of N.C. State University after a single quarter. Gardner contends that, after serving in the U. S. Army, he enrolled at N. C. State and completed three years.

In the early fifties, as in other eras, young men who didn't take well to academics and who didn't move directly into a trade or occupation of some type, joined the Army. Gardner, after faltering early at N. C. State University, joined the U. S. Army. He served three years and attained the rank of Private First Class. Apparently, he and the army meshed no better than he and higher education.

After his discharge, Gardner returned to Rocky Mount where a place was found for him in the family business. Political literature of later times describes Gardner as an executive with the family Dairy. Acquaintances, however, mostly remember young Gardner driving an ice cream truck, peddling popsicles to sweaty youngsters through Rocky Mount neighborhoods.

Members of family firms often are given menial jobs in order to properly train them for leadership roles later in life. That might have been the elder Gardner's objective when he assigned his oldest son to peddle ice cream.

Whatever his status at his father's dairy, his family connection, social station and personal charm were sufficient for him to successfully court the beautiful and gracious Marie, daughter of Arthur L. Tyler.

In the years that were to follow, Gardner and his wife established a home and began to have children. Gardner was doing what he had been conditioned to do by society. He had married well, and was on his way to producing fine children.

He had not, however, "taken hold and made something of himself."

The pressure, however, was clearly building -- from several sources. As the oldest son of a successful businessman, Gardner was challenged by society and by his own inner self to at least achieve a level of success comparable to his father's. As the husband of a woman whose father was exceptionally successful, Gardner was challenged to provide for her in a manner at least equal to that provided by her father. As a child of some privilege, he was schooled in the maxim that "much is expected of those to whom much is given." Gardner acquaintances recall that Gardner seemed to be searching for something he could do on his own.

To those who knew him well, Gardner wasn't a hard worker. Moreover, he did not seem to have a goal about which he could be enthusiastic -- much less passionate.

"Jim always looked for the easy way," says boyhood pal Mack Pearsall. "He just wasn't the kind to get involved. I don't know that he was ever involved in civic or service clubs at all. He didn't seem to be committed to doing things for the community. Around here, it is fairly widespread knowledge that the Gardners are takers, not givers." says Pearsall.

A former member of the Board of Trustees of North Carolina Wesleyan College for nearly two decades, recalls that Gardner never gave a dime to Rocky Mount's major institution of higher education.

Wesleyan College is the best example of civic pride in Rocky Mount, says the former board member who asked not to be identified in order to save the school possible repercussions, "It is the one thing that cuts across religion, politics, everything. It is a rallying point in Rocky Mount. Everybody who is anybody is asked to do something at some time for Wesleyan and Jim Gardner has never done anything.

"If you find somebody in Rocky Mount who doesn't do

something for Wesleyan, you'll find he doesn't do anything for anyone anywhere," said the former trustee. "I'm not aware of a single thing he has ever done for Wesleyan or ever done in his home town to indicate that he cares about his community. This says more about his character than his bad business deals, his bad loans from SBA or anything else."

In the late 1960s with school integration becoming a certainty, a number of well connected people in Rocky Mount joined together to organize the Rocky Mount Academy, a private secondary school that would provide educational refuge for the children of affluent whites.

At the time of the organization, one of the principal voices in favor of the private school was Gardner. Gardner's pledge of financial assistance was among the largest made by any citizen of the area. After the school was established, Gardner sent his children there, but, others who were involved in the establishment of the Rocky Mount Academy recall that Gardner never made good on his pledge. A member of the Board of Directors of the Rocky Mount Academy recalls that Gardner's pledge was written off as uncollectible.

A former legislator from Edgecombe County, remembers that Gardner seemed strongly committed to pleasing wife, Marie. "Those of us who knew him used to joke that Gardner's main occupation was making Marie happy. She was the one with the fortune. As long as Marie was happy with him, Gardner was free to do many things he, otherwise, would not be able to do.

"I don't ever recall having a discussion with Jim Gardner about ideas. I can't recall any idea that he ever expressed that appeared to be original," recalls the former legislator.

Apparently Gardner and his ideas pleased Marie. The couple has enjoyed what appears to be a rock solid marriage over more than three decades. Despite criticism of his politics, business practices, administration of the office of Lieutenant Governor and debating styles, Gardner has escaped even the whisper of marital discord or scandal. Most people who know him say Gardner is a devoted husband, father, and grandfather.

Marie Gardner appears to be a traditional southern woman, accustomed to tending to husband, children, and other family issues. She professes no interest in public life, claims no expertise on the issues, and probably would prefer that her husband avoid what she considers to be the "dreary business" of politics.

Jack Hawke, chairman of the North Carolina Republican Party and a long time friend and associate of Jim Gardner, recalls a conversation in the Gardner home in which Marie Gardner forcefully asserted herself.

It was at the end of Gardner's term in Congress when he was confronted with facing incumbent Congressman L. H. Fountain because of redistricting by the General Assembly.

Gardner was considering the possibility of running for governor in 1968.

"Marie had never been fond of his job in Washington in the first place," recalls Hawke. "The children were quite young then. She is a strong family person. In fact, Mrs. Tyler, Marie's mother, was an invalid during her last years and she lived with Jim and Marie.

"Jim was discussing the choices of running for Congress, and if he won, having to move to Washington, or winning the Governor's race and having to move into the mansion in Raleigh.

"You can do whatever you want to do, Jim," Hawke recalls Marie as stating, "but the children and I are staying in Rocky Mount." They did.

Decades later, Marie Gardner has more enthusiasm for her husband's political ambitions that she did early on, recalls Hawke. She still doesn't like campaigning.

In an interview with The News and Observer shortly after the election of Gardner as the first Republican Lieutenant Governor in the 20th century, Mrs. Gardner said she avoided campaigning because of her fear of public speaking and distaste for crowds. She explained that she was traumatized by a professor during a course she took in public speaking at the University of North Carolina at Chapel Hill.

Gardner's campaign advisers have been concerned that Mrs. Gardner's reluctance to take to the stump in behalf of her husband might hurt his candidacy. She thinks not. She admits that she wasn't thrilled when he announced his candidacy for the U. S. Congress in 1964, or by his subsequent campaigns in 1966, 1968, and 1972. In 1988, when Gardner returned to politics after nearly 20 years, she was fearful that the long string of business failures that he had presided over would be used against him. They were, and quite likely will be every time he might seek public office.

The Gardner's three children are all grown up now. They have two daughters, Beth, 33, Terry, 29, and a son, Chris, 26. They also have three grandchildren, a fact Gardner uses in his political advertising.

One of Gardner's earliest supporters in the media was Jesse Helms, who as operations manager and chief editorialist for WRAL Television in Raleigh and editorial commentator for a chain of radio stations known as the Tobacco Radio Network, praised Gardner frequently during his initial campaign against the veteran Harold Cooley who after many years in Congress, had developed an obtuse political personality aggravated by a kind of rigid arrogance.

The degree of mentoring which Helms might have provided to Gardner is unknown. However, Gardner has developed a personality comparable in many ways to now Senator Helms.

In most of his personal dealings, Helms is unfailingly courteous to all comers, helpful to constituents of whatever political persuasion and cordial in his correspondence and other communications. In politics, however, he adopts a take-no-prisoner attitude and marches across the political landscape, slashing and burning with high velocity rhetoric.

Gardner has the same dual sides. Many people will comment on his personal thoughtfulness and cordiality. Politically, he is a strident idealogue who was among the first candidates to use the tools of mass communications in what we now call negative advertising.

In his formative years, there are no apparent patterns of behavior or unusual episodes that define Gardner's character. It is in his maturity--when he should have had the will and the wisdom to succeed--that Gardner failed--again and again.

IV

The Hardee's Story

Gardner frequently cites Hardee's as the best example of his business experience. He says he co-founded the second largest fast-food chain in America and trumpets this achievement in campaign speeches and advertising as a major reason why the people of North Carolina should elect him Governor.

Gardner also says he once headed Hardee's. Speaking to some 500 of the state's most prominent business, education and government leaders on January 10, 1992 Gardner said: "What I have tried to do is take my business experience because that is the end result of what we do with education in this state.

"A former company that I headed up in Rocky Mount is still based there employs 15,000 people in the state of North Carolina today, 149,000 people across this country. And I'm talking about Hardee's Food Systems."

On July 1, 1992, Gardner released a biographical sketch of

himself in which he stated under a heading of Career Highlights the following: "*Bought a single hamburger stand with a friend in 1962 and built it into Hardee's Food Systems. Today, Hardee's is a $3 billion international industry employing thousands of North Carolinians.*"

All the facts in that statement are technically correct, but the truth of Hardee's founding and growth is a substantially different story than the "facts" which Gardner lists.

Gardner's assertion that he and partner Leonard Rawls, a certified public accountant, together started a franchise sales effort which they called Hardee's Food Systems Inc. is correct. However, their venture evolved directly from the Hardee's hamburger concept, developed solely by Wilber Hardee. In claiming credit for the venture, Gardner never mentions Hardee, the true founder of the restaurant chain, nor does he delineate the difference between Hardee's restaurants and the franchise sales plan which was named Hardee's Food Systems to capitalize on the Hardee's concept.

Wilber Hardee, the man whose name adorns the sign above the some 3,600 Hardee's Restaurants, adamantly denies that Gardner had anything to do with building the first Hardee's Restaurant.

The 73-year-old Wilber Hardee recalls that Gardner was still driving an ice cream truck for his father's dairy nearly a year after the original Hardee's Restaurant was operating profitably in Greenville, North Carolina.

"If Jim Gardner says he founded Hardee's, he is lying," said Hardee. "I founded Hardee's. Jim Gardner and Leonard Rawls came along and tricked me out of my store and my name.

"When I pass by a Hardee's sign, I feel like it's still mine. I ought to have benefitted more from their success."

Hardee is not as bitter now about his brief partnership with Gardner as he was years ago. He attributes his change of mind to a religious conversion which has brought a willingness to forgive to his heart.

Would Wilber Hardee trust Jim Gardner again?
No!

Hardee is a soft-spoken man, easygoing and eager to trust his fellowman. A native of rural Pitt County, just east of

Greenville, Hardee has recently begun another business. He opened the first of what he hopes will become a national franchise chain of American Barbecue restaurants. The flagship restaurant is in the little town of Grifton, North Carolina.

Grifton, with a population of 2,393, is located midway between Greenville and Kinston. Hardee's American Barbecue is off the four-lane highway right in the middle of town, across from the Police Department in what used to be a Fast Fare Store.

That's part of his strategy for making this company successful.

"There are some 125 empty Fast Fare store buildings in North Carolina right now," Hardee said. "You can rent them for a fraction of what it costs to build a new building. They're perfect for this kind of use."

Hardee is excited about the challenge ahead of him, of building another successful fast food chain, and he is confident his new venture will succeed. Behind this effort is more than a year's work devoted to building special gas-fired cookers for both pork and chicken barbecue which allow the food to be cooked quickly and efficiently but with the distinct flavor of hickory coals.

He envisions people enjoying his barbecue all over America within the next few years and he hopes American Barbecue will offer him the chance to succeed that he lost when he was forced out of Hardee's.

Hardee, a self-made man who quit school in the 7th grade, has had a special knack for the restaurant business ever since he went to work at 14.

He already had nearly two decades of food service experience when he heard about a new fast-food facility that had opened in Greensboro, then North Carolina's second largest city, located 200 miles west of Greenville.

He went to see the first McDonalds to come to central North Carolina and was truly fascinated with the concept and its potential.

"I watched them for an hour and figured they took in more than $100, selling 15-cent hamburgers. I never imagined you could make $100 an hour selling hamburgers for 15 cents."

Hardee went back to Greenville and built himself a restaurant selling hamburgers for 15 cents. He made good hamburgers and still earned a gross profit of nine cents each. He put his name on the restaurant. This was the restaurant concept that was to grow over the years and to be known all over the world as "Hardee's."

Hardee was proud of his restaurant the day Leonard Rawls, an accountant from Washington, North Carolina, stopped in and said he had noticed how much business the little restaurant was drawing and suggested this might be the kind of business which could be built lots of places.

Rawls, said his friend in Rocky Mount, Jim Gardner, could sell ice cream cones to Eskimos. Together they could make a fortune. And the name "Hardee" would be a household name all over America.

"I trusted them two boys," Hardee recalled with disappointment but no bitterness left in his voice. "I trusted them like my brothers."

Hardee agreed to go in business with Gardner and Rawls. The two partners built a second Hardee's, this one in Rocky Mount where Gardner lived. It was as successful as the first one had been in Greenville.

Then came the transaction that would cut Wilber Hardee out of the company and go on to make millions on his idea and his name.

One night in January of 1961 Rawls visited Hardee at his hamburger restaurant in Greenville and suggested they go out, get a steak and have a drink. Over dinner and several drinks Rawls said he had an agreement for Hardee to sign. Nothing special, just a document so they could get started big time in the business that was going to make all of them rich. After dinner, Rawls took Hardee to the office he shared with Gardner, where Gardner and their attorney were waiting. It was nearly midnight, Hardee recalled.

Hardee looked briefly at the document, already written and typed, and initialed his acceptance. He had gotten to like these men. They were friendly and good-natured like himself, he thought, so there was no reason to bother his lawyer with this matter.

He learned later that the document he signed gave complete control of the company to Gardner and Rawls.

The next day after Hardee signed the agreement, his two new partners called a meeting of the Board of Directors and voted to start selling franchises themselves, cutting Hardee out of any benefit of future sales.

"I took the agreement to my lawyer and he told me I'd been had," Hardee said. *"I knew it, too."*

Hardee kept his restaurant in Greenville for a couple of months and then sold it to Gardner and Rawls for $20,000.

In a newspaper interview in 1988, Gardner denied Hardee's allegation. "We begged him not to get out of Hardee's. I've never heard one word of this," Gardner was quoted in an article in the News and Observer.

"Jim Gardner stole my company and he stole my name," Hardee said. *"You ask me if I trust him? You ask me if I believe he ought to be Governor of North Carolina. Well, let me answer you this way. I don't hold a grudge against any man. Since, I accepted Christ as my Savior, there hasn't been room in by heart for anger toward anyone. If Jim Gardner came to me today and asked me to forgive him, I would do so. But I don't think he will. I don't think he is that kind of man."*

How does he feel whenever he passes a Hardee's restaurant or a Hardees billboard with its bright orange letters?

"I feel like it's still mine," Hardee said. *"It seems like it should still belong to me."*

A document published by the Public Relations Office of Hardee's Food Systems, Inc., in 1990, commemorating the company's 30th anniversary confirms many of the facts which Hardee tells about the establishment of the company.

The company version acknowledges that the original Hardee's restaurant was begun by Wilber Hardee and not Jim Gardner. However, the company misspelled his name. They spelled it "Wilbur" throughout the entire document.

Not much is said about Gardner. He is mentioned only four times in the lengthy statement and not at all after page one. The company explains Gardner's departure tersely, "Jim Gardner served as the company's first executive vice president until 1966 when he left to pursue a career in government."

Leonard Rawls, the document also notes, served as Hardees first president and chief executive officer until 1975. If Hardees official history is correct, Gardner is incorrect when he contends that he once "headed" the fast-food chain. Hardee's corporation records, on file at the Secretary of State's office, confirm that Gardner was never president of Hardee's Food Systems, Inc.

The launching of restaurants such as Hardees and a score of other fast-food restaurants was perhaps inevitable.

Changing demographics -- the entry of large numbers of young people into high school and college, swelling numbers of young parents with children, the expansion of the interstate highway system, the increasing role of the automobile in the retail scheme -- all of these factors created a ready market for inexpensive food appealing to the young, the hurried, and those with underdeveloped and unsophisticated dining habits.

Emulating the pioneering McDonald's chain was fairly easy.

Creating the fast-food chain consisted of locating likely spots, doing traffic and customer counts and, if the counts were high enough, purchasing land and plopping down another hamburger stand. It was not the cutting edge technology. Success in this venture required no creative breakthroughs, but the way it was practiced by Leonard Rawls and Jim Gardner, the concept was very profitable.

Very early, Gardner and Rawls decided to copy another successful McDonald idea -- to franchise their hamburger stands to others. Under the plan, the Hardees team would agree to sell an individual the right to build and operate a Hardee's restaurant. For a significant fee and a continuing share of income, the owner of the franchise would receive the benefits of previous Hardee's experience, bulk purchases and advertising.

It was in selling these franchises that Gardner was most adept.

The importance of selling Hardee's hamburger franchises should not be minimized in the establishment of a successful fast-food chain that has grown to be a significant worldwide factor. It is the one and only business venture in which Gardner has achieved success. In the wheeling and dealing that followed that initial success of Hardee's, many people played key roles. While Gardner's role in the initial selling effort was major, his subsequent role in the management of the company was minor.

While he occupied a position of leadership, the company was in almost constant litigation. His leadership role at Hardee's was brief and when he left, the company sued him for a substantial amount of money.

The resolution of that suit remains something of a mystery. Records pertaining to it have been removed from the Nash County Courthouse.

While he was in a position of leadership, Gardner's actions frequently landed Hardee's in court. A man who had sold a lot on which a Hardee's restaurant was to be built sued to force payment for the property. Bo Thorpe, the band leader, sued to recover payment for public relations work.

Unauthorized Use of Advertising

One of the most embarrassing legal actions against Hardee's resulting from a Gardner decision occurred when a New York firm, Phil Davis Musical Enterprises, sued the company for unauthorized use of advertising materials.

The Davis firm sued Hardees for $100,000 in U.S. Eastern District Court in Wilson, charging that Hardee's had used four advertising jingles without paying for them. The jingles promoted the theme, "Head for Hardee's."

Hardees had obtained the tapes from the advertising firm of Harry Gianaris and Associates of Charleston, South Carolina, who had been solicited by Gardner to suggest a new advertising concept and "catchy" jingle for the company.

Davis testified in court that in response to a request from Gianaris, his firm spent a week developing the Hardee's advertising materials and had prepared an audio tape to demonstrate the concept and provide a preliminary rendition of the commercials.

Davis testified that his firm routinely charged a fee for the creative and technical work involved in creating the commercials based on their use. If the Hardee's materials were not used, Gianaris was to pay $350 which represented just the cost of getting the advertising concepts recorded on audio tape.

When Gianaris made his sales presentation to Hardee's, Gardner asked him to leave the demonstration tapes with the firm so that other members of the organization might review them for possible use.

Reluctantly, Gianaris complied with Gardner's request. Later, he learned that his sales presentation had not been accepted and that his firm would not acquire the Hardee's advertising account. Instead, Hardee's retained the Lewis Advertising Agency of Rocky Mount.

Gianaris billed Hardee's for $350 for the cost of recording the commercials on audio tape. He said his invoice clearly indicated that the $350 did not include any rights or license to use the commercials on radio or in other media.

Gianaris said Hardee's paid the $350 invoice and made no indication that the material would be used. A year later, he was startled to hear the commercials on a Charleston, South Carolina television station.

Hardee's used the commercials on radio and incorporated them into television, print and outdoor advertising--without payment to Davis or Gianaris.

Gianaris notified the Phil Davis firm of Hardee's use of the material and the Davis firm sued. When the case came to court, Gene Lewis provided damaging testimony against Gardner. He said Gardner instructed him to use the commercials although he had advised Gardner that Hardee's was not authorized to use them without payment. Lewis testified he warned Gardner that Hardee's would expose itself to liability if the company used the tapes without payment.

Gardner ignored the warning and instructed Lewis to use the tapes.

Gardner did not appear in court to defend his position. Instead, he submitted an affidavit in which he denied any wrong-doing. He contended that the $350 payment made to Gianaris was for the right to use the materials and cited as supporting evidence the label on the tapes which read "Hardee's Demo Tape."

On November 15, the jury returned a unanimous verdict in favor of Phil Davis in the amount of $16,750. In doing so, it had to disbelieve the sworn statement of Gardner.

The jury also forbade Hardee's from making any further use of the materials incorporating the phrase "Head for Hardee's." Hardee's paid the judgment the same day.

V

Politics
A Fire In His Belly

When Gardner first stepped into the political arena in 1964, he was clothed in a mantle of success. He claimed, and no one disputed, a primary role in the founding of a vibrantly successful business.

At age 32, Gardner looked like a political candidate from Hollywood's central casting. Tall, trim, handsome, articulate and aggressive, he appeared to be a man of substance. A hint of gray lightened his temples, and, thus, he appeared to have been tempered by time just enough to have acquired mature wisdom.

No one thought to pose a question of utmost gravity: How did success as a salesman of Hardee hamburger franchises qualify a largely uneducated young man of limited experience to deal with the diverse issues of a nation less than two decades removed from a World War, already embroiled in another shooting war and confronting what appeared to be the implacable foe of worldwide communism?

Gardner gave the appearance of being up to the task.

Appearances were deceiving. Gardner had not been tested by the fires of adversity. He had not achieved character by overcoming obstacles without sacrificing principle. He had not come to conclusions about the great philosophical issues of the times through dedicated scholarship or through the testing of his own convictions. He mouthed certainties with the glibness of a sportscaster reciting baseball scores, but to the careful listener his pronouncements came through as a synthetic synthesis of other people's platitudes. Events and the future course of his life support the thesis that whatever wisdom Gardner possessed in 1964 was clearly second-hand.

At the base of Gardner's political ascendancy rests a fascinating mystery. From easy-going, laid-back popsicle-peddling Democrat, Gardner underwent some kind of personal and political metamorphosis that transformed him into an articulate, persuasive Republican advocating the philosophy of John Birch, George Wallace and Barry Goldwater.

What, indeed, turned a 32-year-old purveyor of cheap hamburger, french fries, soft drinks, apple pies and milkshakes into a Republican pit bull spouting forth simplistic solutions to serious economic and social problems of the times that came to be labeled as new wave Republicanism? What, indeed, caused the changes in Gardner?

Many in Rocky Mount, Gardner's hometown, recall that Gardner and several other business and social associates went en masse to the board of elections and changed their party registration from Democrat to Republican.

In this time of political disarray, declaring yourself a Republican is perfectly respectable, but before two-party politics had come of age in North Carolina and the South, such a move in Eastern North Carolina carried both financial and social risks. Some may call Gardner's decision courageous; others may say it was reckless.

Some traditional Democrats in North Carolina who have gone over to the Republican side contend that they never left the party, but rather the Democratic party left them. There is a rationale for this perception.

Under the heavy hands of Lyndon Johnson, the Democratic

Party espoused a political philosophy that was perceived in a very negative manner by many voters who had traditionally voted the straight Democratic ticket. The essence of the new perception is described by Thomas Byrne Edsall, co-author of <u>Chain Reaction, the Impact of Race, Rights and Taxes on American Politics</u>.

Instead of being seen as advancing the economic well being of all voters, including white mainstream working and middle-class voters, liberalism and the Democratic Party came to be perceived in key sectors of the electorate, as promoting the establishment of new rights and government guarantees for previously marginalized, stigmatized, or historically disenfranchised groups, often at the expense of traditional constituencies.

In some respects, wrote Edsall, "The Democratic Party became the advocate and champion of a liberal agenda institutionalized by the Warren Court." During the Warren years, the U. S. Supreme Court handed down a series of rulings beginning with the *Brown vs. Board of Education* and continuing with the Miranda ruling and other votes that promoted the rights of minorities and infuriated many North Carolinians and other southerners.

The rulings of the Warren Court took from some and gave to others. In the South, those from whom something was taken were mostly white. Those to whom something was given were mostly black.

More than money was at issue. Whites who were reared in a time of racial separation and, who, by culture and conditioning, had come to believe in their own superiority were forced to compromise long-standing values. They had to send their children to integrated schools. Society moved -- sometimes slowly -- but always inexorably toward integration. Whites perceived that they not only had to give up their preferred status, but also were forced to finance the movement with additional taxes.

For many years, the Democratic Party was essentially two parties in North Carolina, one party made up of fiscal and social conservatives, the other comprised of men and women who believed themselves to be more progressive-minded. Tensions between the two branches of the party have often served as checkmates, each on the other, preventing excesses and creating a political climate in which large numbers of middle-ground moderates could be comfortable.

Former President Gerald Ford once said that the one thing Republicans did really well was "lose gracefully." Noting the historic dominance of Democrats in the U. S. House of Representatives where he had served, Ford explained that Republicans had more experience at losing than at winning.

North Carolina Republicans once had a reputation for losing gracefully. The winners of Democratic primaries had for most of the 20th century eased into the governor's office without breaking a sweat during the general election.

In 1964, the year Jim Gardner decided to enter the political arena, Republican Robert Gavin faced Dan Moore for governor. Gavin's worst criticism of Moore was that Moore was not campaigning very aggressively.

In a speech in Mount Airy, Moore defended himself by saying that he had been campaigning hard. The mild-mannered mountain man chided his Republican opponent on Gavin's lack of experience. So unexpected were Moore's remarks that some news reporters wrote that Moore "tore into" his opponent. By contemporary standards in which hit-and-run attack TV ads dominate, the exchange was a love-in.

Indeed, in other statements during the 1964 campaign, Republican Gavin promised that if elected he would try to persuade Democrat Moore to accept a job in his administration.

The year 1964 marked a turning point in political civility in the nation and in North Carolina.

When Gardner announced his candidacy against the veteran Harold Cooley, it was apparent from his manner and the tone of his remarks that Gardner was committed to winning, that he had no intention of losing gracefully.

Gardner's entry into politics in North Carolina coincided with the nomination of Barry Goldwater as the Republican candidate for president. The presidential campaign pitting liberal Johnson against the conservative Goldwater set in motion at the presidential level the most ideological confrontation of the 20th century.

The ideology emanated from the major political issue of the times, the Johnson-sponsored Civil Rights Act of 1964. Until

1964, the emphasis of government in the civil rights arena was to seek to guarantee minorities, principally black people, the fundamental rights that white people enjoyed, to open doors and to grant access to opportunities that had been denied previously because of race.

The Civil Rights Act of 1964 sought not only to provide access to opportunity, but, insofar as possible, to guarantee the equal rights for black people.

At the national level, the Republicans, under Goldwater's leadership, publicly and adamantly opposed the Civil Rights Act of 1964. Goldwater's candidacy energized Southern whites who were concerned about racial integration and the growing movement for more rights for black people, and for more taxation of white people to pay for what they perceived to be special benefits and privileges for black people. To a large degree, this newly energized bloc of voters had not been active participants in previous elections.

Gardner quickly sought to identify himself with Goldwater, and, thus, to capture the significant bloc of dissatisfied voters.

President Johnson was able to define the national campaign as a War vs. Peace issue, with himself cast as the champion of peace and Goldwater as a somewhat hysterical, unbalanced warmonger who wanted "to lob a nuke into the men's room at the Kremlin."

The emphasis on war and peace in the national election muted to some degree the issue of civil rights in North Carolina. Gardner mainly waged war on Cooley's record, depicting him as arrogant and out of touch with the needs of North Carolina and the district. To some extent, Cooley, who held the powerful chairmanship of the House Agricultural Committee, was arrogant. After many terms of office, he had come to believe that he was immune to voter rejection.

Gardner went for Cooley where the veteran congressman should have been invulnerable -- on agricultural issues.

Gardner also sought to link Cooley and U. S. Secretary of Agriculture Orville Freeman as two liberals who favored recognition of Red China, opposed inspection of nuclear facilities in the Soviet Union, favored 'appeasement' of Cuba's Castro, socialized medicine and the abolition of the House Un-American

Activities Committee.

Cooley responded by inviting Secretary Freeman to come to North Carolina to tell farmers how important Cooley was to the success of the commodities program in North Carolina.

Goldwater came to North Carolina, too, but he proved to have no coattails at all for Tar Heel candidates. He seemed to have no understanding of the state's tobacco and peanut allotment programs, and in a comical gaffe, said he had once "shaved in peanut butter."

Most of the debate between the two candidates was presented to the public through news coverage and newspaper advertisements. The advent of the ugly TV attack ad was still almost a decade in the future.

During the early days of the 1964 campaign, Gardner and other Republicans felt that Democratic Gubernatorial Candidate Dan Moore would distance himself so far from Lyndon Johnson that he would make it acceptable for Democrats to vote Republican. Dan Moore surprised many by enthusiastically endorsing Johnson, travelling with him in the State and unifying the Democratic Party.

In the same year that Martin Luther King won the Nobel Peace Prize, Nikita S. Khrushchev was deposed in the Soviet Union, Red China exploded its first nuclear device and Lyndon Johnson's top aide Walter Jenkins was charged with homosexual solicitation in a Washington rest room, Gardner experienced his first bitter taste of political defeat.

Gardner vowed to return. A fire had been ignited in his belly that would not be extinguished by political defeat or business humiliation.

The 1966 Campaign For Congress: How Sweet It Was!

In the period between his defeat in 1964 and the beginning of the 1966 campaign for Congress, Jim Gardner was elected chairman of the North Carolina Republican Party, thus gaining credibility with Republicans across North Carolina.

As he had promised, however, Gardner, in 1966, threw his hat back into the political ring in North Carolina's Fourth District. He seemed more determined than ever to depose the venerable, but vulnerable, Congressman Harold Cooley.

The off-year U. S. Senate race pitted businessman John Shallcross against the incumbent Senator B. Everett Jordan. Shallcross went down in dignified defeat as was the customary fate of most other Republicans in North Carolina during that era.

One of the issues of the times much in the news was an assignment given to students at UNC-Chapel Hill by a young part-time English instructor to write a theme on seduction. The public debate on what now appears to be a trivial matter is indicative of the tenor and tone of the times of the mid 60s in North Carolina.

Governor Dan Moore had solidified his position as one of North Carolina's most popular governors. The Ku Klux Klan was rumbling in the wake of Lyndon Johnson's persistent pursuit of expanded civil rights for Negroes. Johnson's Vietnam war policies were beginning to arouse concern which he defused somewhat by proclaiming that the nation could afford both "guns and butter," a now discredited catch phrase of the 60s.

On the surface times seemed tranquil. Just beneath the surface, however, were the issues that were later to erupt into riots, wholesale civil disobedience and urban discord.

Gardner's hard-charging campaign of 1964 had won him many friends and admirers. In 1966 he still held on to the core of his 1964 support -- those dissatisfied, disaffected Tar Heels who were opposed to the pace of racial desegregation and the liberalism of the Lyndon Johnson presidency.

Indeed, the Gardner constituency was a strange mixture. Gardner was the favorite of well-to-do conservative whites. He also had strong support among younger white voters who were becoming established in business and the professions. He was highly regarded by blue collar and rural males who were sometimes referred to as "rednecks." His constituency also included many who had continued to believe the conventional wisdom of the Kennedy mystique that youth, physical attractiveness and glibness somehow translated into expertise in governance.

In 1966, Gardner's hair was a tad grayer around the temples than in 1964, but he had honed a finer edge to his political rhetoric, and the experience of the 1964 campaign had given him confidence.

On the political stump, confidence became a Gardner hallmark. From the outset of the campaign, he predicted victory. He produced polls that showed him gaining on, even overtaking, Cooley. Gardner even attracted liberals.

In 1964, I. Beverly Lake, a Democratic candidate for governor who later was appointed to the North Carolina Supreme Court had described the University of North Carolina, which he viewed as a citadel of liberalism, as a "pink pimple on the red rump of communism." Even so, Gardner had a local and vocal support group among those "left-leaning" students and faculty at Chapel Hill. Political pundits could not readily explain Gardner's appeal to what appeared to be an ever-growing base of support.

Cooley had confronted another problem: He had been ripped and torn in the 1964 Democratic primary that pitted him against aggressive Mayne Albright, one-time candidate for the Democratic nomination for Governor.

In 1948, Albright had been the spoiler in the campaign that enabled Kerr Scott to call for a runoff against favorite Charles Johnson and, thus, to change the history of North Carolina politics. Early in that 1948 contest, Albright was believed to be the real challenger to Johnson, who had served as state treasurer for many years. Johnson was a member of the traditional, conservative wing of the Democratic Party and, thus, was expected to follow Gregg Cherry into the Governor's office with little trouble.

Albright began touring the state in a trailer, delivering fiery stump speeches that delighted many and appalled some. As the three-way race progressed, Scott, with a campaign for getting the farmer out of the mud, expanding rural electrification and, in general, making life better for rural folk, surged ahead of Albright.

In the 1948 Democratic Primary, Albright came in third, permitting second-place finisher Scott to demand a runoff with the first place finisher, Johnson. Scott won the runoff, upsetting the old Guard Democratic machine for the first time in a generation. Albright returned to the practice of law and had maintained a low profile until the 1964 primary.

Albright entered the 1964 campaign fully prepared. In speech after speech, Albright ripped into Cooley's record, his personality, his performance in office and the issue that troubled the voters the most, Cooley's arrogance.

Cooley had survived the 1964 assault by Gardner shaken, but still confident that his hold on the electorate was solidified by his position as Chairman of the House Agriculture Committee. He had failed to realize that in the changing demographics of the Fourth District agriculture was not the sacred cow it had been for so many decades.

In the 1966 Democratic primary, Cooley confronted two more strong opponents, Bill Creech and Columbus Tart. Bob men campaigned aggressively, reopening the wounds that had not fully healed from the Albright and Gardner attacks of 1964. In 1966 Gardner's principal task was to deliver the coup de grace, which he did with enthusiasm. By storming the district with numerous news conferences in which he would deliver verbal blasts at Cooley, by exuding a hard-edged youthful vigor, by reducing complex issues to simplistic slogans, Gardner presented a compelling contrast to the aging, arrogant Cooley, who mostly seemed embittered that he was having to campaign at all.

There was a meanness about the campaign in the fourth district that disconcerted many voters. Gardner seemed personally angry at Cooley, holding him responsible for events over which no individual Congressman could have exercised much, if any, influence. Gardner seemed to actually enjoy his systematic destruction of Cooley, who, despite some personal peccadillos, had for many years represented North Carolina, the Fourth District and particularly the state's agricultural interests with distinction.

Gardner had Cooley on the ropes from round one, and probably could have won the campaign easily by taking only the high road. He chose to be confrontational for the sake of confrontation. He attacked Cooley time and again when he would have fared just as well by running a positive campaign.

In the media, the Fourth District congressional campaign was waged mostly in the newspapers. Gardner ran a series of ads presenting himself as a co-founder of Hardees, a matter of dispute in the decades to follow, and as a civic and business leader.

In one newspaper ad, Gardner listed numerous civic clubs in which he claimed membership. Congressman I. T. "Tim" Valentine, then chairman of the Democratic Party and a resident of Nashville, neighboring town to Gardner's hometown of Rocky Mount, called Gardner's hand on his assertion of civic leadership. Valentine said Gardner had joined many of the clubs just to fatten his resume, but that for the most of his life he had not been a participant in the civic life of his community. Other acquaintances of Gardner confirm Valentine's contention.

Gardner, recognizing that he was better at debating than the aging Cooley, constantly baited Cooley to debate him on television.

Cooley steadfastly refused, but the two candidates finally came together at a political forum sponsored by students at N. C. State University. The event was not a formal debate, but merely provided a forum for the two candidates to appear together and make speeches. What made the event different was that the area's two principal television stations, WRAL, and WTVD, both filmed the presentations by Cooley and Gardner.

Unknown to Cooley, Gardner had his political and media consultant, Earl Cox, purchase the film from WRAL-TV. Cox proceeded to cut and edit the raw footage into what appeared to be a debate between the two candidates. Gardner's campaign then purchased time to broadcast the doctored film.

In the carefully edited version of the confrontation, Cooley was completely demolished by Gardner. He appeared to be confused, inarticulate and sometimes out of touch with reality. Gardner came across as bright, quick-witted, in command of the facts and totally confident.

Possibly, Gardner would have appeared more effective in the confrontation even if the film had not been doctored. Gardner took no chances. He shaped the film to his best and Cooley's worst advantage and aired the result as a balanced presentation.

Cooley was outraged. He threatened to seek sanctions against the Federal Communication license of WRAL-TV, causing some nervousness on the part of the station, although its management refused to admit fault.

Had Cooley been re-elected and continued to hold his power in Washington, it is possible that he could have created real trouble for WRAL-TV. In the aftermath of the controversy WRAL-TV adopted a policy that prohibited the sale of news film or tape to political candidates.

In the last days of the campaign of 1966, it was evident that Cooley was in trouble. Gardner produced polls showing that he was ahead. Traditional Democrats did not want to believe that a young political upstart could unseat one of the nation's most influential Congressman.

A week before the November election, the weather took a bizarre and nasty turn. Tornadoes and high winds ripped across much of the Fourth Congressional District, and unseasonable snow blanketed parts of the State.

The storm did not compare with the electoral storm that occurred a week later when voters of the Fourth District buried Harold Cooley politically in a landslide for Gardner.

Gardner's exhilaration was evident when he jubilantly proclaimed, "How Sweet It Is!" when he claimed victory.

VI

In Congress But Seldom There

Gardner was elected to Congress during a time of great turbulence in this country. The Vietnam War was beginning to escalate in January of 1967 when the dapper, young hamburger tycoon took his oath of office. Unknown to most people, a social revolution was gathering steam.

Gardner went to Washington backed by a landslide victory and the best wishes of just about everyone, even by those who had opposed his candidacy. The times called out for fresh thinking, for a Congressman committed to excellence. Gardner failed the test--miserably.

In his two years in Congress, Gardner amassed one of the worst attendance records in the history of the nation. He perceived the normal intercourse between his constituency and his office as pressure tactics, and his letters to persons in the Fourth District on topics of crucial importance reflected muddled thinking and poor communications skills.

Gardner has never bothered to explain adequately why he

did not attend the sessions of Congress or meetings of the House Committee on Education and Labor which were so important to the needs and opportunities of North Carolina and the South which were just beginning to feel the full impact of school desegregation.

The man who had accused his predecessor of arrogance in office made Harold Cooley's demeanor appear to be humble.

As he geared up his 1968 campaign for Governor, Gardner knew his attendance record in Congress was a potential problem. In a May 20, 1968 letter to C. Whid Powell of Chapel Hill who had inquired about his frequent absences, Gardner wrote:

"My record for the 1st session was 87% and for the current session is 53%. I realize that the latter is very low; however, I have made every effort to work my campaign schedule around my Congressional responsibilities and be present for voting on legislation which I felt to be the most significant for North Carolina."

Gardner's letter indicated that he felt his campaign activities were more important than his duties in Congress. Gardner just didn't like Congress. He simply was not suited to the give-and-take that characterizes that institution. He wanted to be top dog in every situation, and in Congress he was surrounded by hundreds of others who wanted the same thing and were better qualified to capture attention.

Gardner didn't like to play by the Congressional rules. And he didn't. He decided to run for Governor. His opponent in the Republican primary was businessman Jack Stickley, who issued a statement through his campaign manager, on April 2, 1968, accusing Gardner of having ". . . the worst voting record of any North Carolina Congressman."

At that time, Stickley charged Gardner had missed 12 of 38 votes.

In his reply to Stickley, Gardner said:

"I was quite amused to hear the statement made by my opponent's campaign manager concerning his interest in my voting record in Congress.

"First of all, I happen to feel very strongly that a United States Congressman has a definite obligation to spend a larger percentage of his time in his Congressional District, meeting fact (sic) to face with people who have problems. Along these lines, I

have, since my election to Congress, maintained Congressional offices in each of the seven counties in my district. I have also maintained monthly office hours. To my knowledge, this is not being done by any other member of the North Carolina Congressional Delegation.

"It is quite interesting that for 32 years the Fourth Congressional District was represented by a man who thought he should spend all of his time in Washington and none of it in the district. I shall continue to follow this very same policy. I would ask my opponent's campaign manager for the opponent's excuse in missing 41 of 58 votes as a citizen since 1954. I find it most interesting that a man who has never been remotely interested in political activities during the last 14 years would, all of a sudden want to be Governor of North Carolina. I would like to say to the citizens of North Carolina, that I am not a candidate, handpicked by a small group of individuals, but I am running for the Governorship of this state because I feel that I can offer positive programs that will help build a better state for our children in the days to come."

Just two years earlier, candidate Gardner, had accused the veteran incumbent Congressman Harold Cooley of being an absentee Congressman.

Cooley, then serving as the distinguished and powerful Chairman of the House Agriculture Committee actually had a respectable 81% attendance rate in roll call votes.

During his 1966 campaign for the Fourth District, Gardner said that one of his reasons for running was: "*I want to give this district the attention and full time it deserves.*"

Even after announcing his 1968 gubernatorial campaign, Gardner promised that he would continue to be "a full-time" Congressman. He further said, "*I have a strong obligation to fulfill the two years' responsibility to the people who elected me.*"

Stickley pointed out another interesting aspect about Gardner's skimpy voting record. In describing him as a "Tuesday-to-Thursday Congressman," Stickley noted that Gardner "*had the highest absentee rate on Monday and Friday votes of any member of the North Carolina Congressional Delegation in 1967.*"

Throughout the last half of 1968 Gardner's attendance record worsened. The Congressional Quarterly Almanac recorded

Gardner's absences as follows:

1967	1968	67-68 Session
13%	56%	34%

While Gardner's absences were troubling to many, it was his performance as a member of the House Education and Labor Committee that truly shocked constituents.

Education Committee

The young Congressman was so proud of his assignment to the Committee on Education and Labor that he dispatched a special press release from his office on January 12, 1968, announcing his appointment.

"I am grateful and thankful for being named to what I consider one of the most important committees in Washington," Gardner said.

"I am particularly pleased to be serving on a committee charged with the responsibility of handling legislation affecting the entire sphere of education. I feel much can be done to improve and meet the growing need for better educational opportunities."

The release went on to explain that the committee, founded in 1947, dealt with the legislation covering the entire field of education, labor, child labor laws, labor standards, labor statistics, mediation and arbitration of labor disputes, importation of foreign laborers under contract, the school lunch program, U. S. Employees Compensation Commission, vocational rehabilitation, wage and hour laws and the welfare of minors.

In the spring of 1968, Gardner reiterated the importance of his membership on the House Education and Labor Committee.

Writing in his 62nd weekly newspaper column, Gardner said: *"The Special Subcommittee on Education of the House Education and Labor Committee, of which I am a member, held hearings on the Higher Education Amendments HR 15067, from February 6 through March 8. Since completion of the hearings, we have been meeting in executive sessions to 'mark up' or rewrite this bill. Our revisions are based, to a great extent, on the testimony which we have heard from private citizens, educators, various educational organizations, government officials and others as well as the information that the Committee investigators have been able to secure.*

"On April 23rd we reported out a clean bill on Title IV of the Amendments which deals only with student assistance. . . . . The clean bill which I am sponsoring with a number of my colleagues on the Education and Labor Committee makes only technical changes in the original provisions of Title IV of HR 15067 and provides for no overall increase in authorization."

He went on to explain that no additional money was needed since the initial appropriation had not been used up in the previous year.

And finally, the column concluded:

"These proposals reflect the high priority being given student assistance as compared to the lower priority being given programs for construction of academic and housing facilities for colleges and universities. In a period of budget stringency, I feel that strict budget priorities must be imposed and must be adhered to. I tend to agree that the greater need is in the area of student assistance rather than in construction and equipment plans. Sincerely, James C. Gardner."

This column was sent, as were all his weekly columns, to news media in the seven counties (Chatham, Montgomery, Moore, Nash, Orange, Randolph and Wake) of the Fourth District.

The column appears to be structured so as to indicate that Gardner was hard at work on education matters in the spring of 1968, even in the middle of his campaign for Governor. That was obviously the intent of a carefully worded document.

However, during the entire year of 1968, Gardner did not attend a single meeting of the House Education and Labor Committee. Nor did he attend any of the subcommittee meetings.

There were 19 meetings of the House Education and Labor Committee in 1968 and in each of the officially recorded minutes, Gardner is listed as absent. He is also shown absent from each of the subcommittee meetings, even those which he reported to be dutifully at work.

In 1967 the record shows that he attended seven of the committee's 14 meetings.

In his book, A Time To Speak, prepared during his campaign for Governor, a picture of Gardner is shown standing underneath the sign over the door leading to the meeting room of the House Education and Labor Committee.

Posing for that picture, outside the meeting room, was as close as Jim Gardner got to the important education committee during half of his entire term in Congress.

In January of 1968, he replied to a letter received a month earlier from Ben E. Hoffmeyer, then Superintendent of the North Carolina School for the Deaf at Morganton.

Superintendent Hoffmeyer had asked Gardner to support the Senate version of H.R. 7819 which would have brought special help to handicapped children.

In a rambling, almost incoherent letter, Gardner wrote:

"Dear Mr. Hoffmeyer: Thank you for your recent letter concerning the Elementary and Secondary Education Amendments of 1967.

"These amendments were designed to strengthen and improve programs of assistance to elementary and secondary education through advance funding of elementary and secondary schools one year in advance of the year in which they will be obligated. The total authorization of funds for Fiscal 1969 was $9.3 billion.

"One of the new programs included under the Amendments was a program which establishes and operates regional centers for the special education needs of handicapped children.

"I did not support this bill, primarily because of my objection to Federal control over education through the allocation of Federal funds. However, I am pleased with the provisions therein for the handicapped. It is my sincere wish that the provisions contained in these amendments will serve to strengthen and improve our elementary and secondary educational system. Sincerely, James C. Gardner, Member of Congress"

The convoluted syntax of Gardner's letter seemed to say he was for handicapped children, but that he voted against the bill to help them. And even though he voted against their interest, he hoped they would think kindly of him as a friend of the unfortunate.

Social Security

Social Security was an important issue during Gardner's

years in Congress. Gardner didn't approve of President Lyndon Johnson's effort to strengthen the financial stability of the elderly in the last days of their lives. Gardner was often blunt in rejecting constituent requests for increased Social Security payments.

In January of 1968, as he was launching his campaign for Governor, Gardner wrote P. H. Cannads of Hillsborough and provided a view of the Social Security program that reflected a curious mindset.

"The Social Security program," Gardner wrote, "was begun because the fact that so many people did not and would not willingly save a portion of their monthly income towards a retirement fund became a very large and difficult problem. And, unlike your parents, many of these persons had no relatives on which to rely after retirement. Thus rather than let the number of these individuals increase and continue to be dependent on the government, the Social Security program was established."

Gardner apparently disliked the Social Security program but he also realized the jeopardy in which he would place his future political aspirations if he did not show some support for the popular program.

Therefore, in a March 6, 1967, reply to a letter from James Arnold of Hillsborough who sent a petition from several constituents asking that he support President Johnson's proposed 20 percent increase in Social Security benefits, Gardner wrote that he favored a bill which would increase the benefits only six percent. But within the next two weeks, he changed his mind.

On March 20, 1967, Gardner wrote a letter to L. E. Beck of Siler City who also had written to ask the Congressman to vote for the proposed increase.

Gardner wrote: *"As you may realize the inadequacy of Social Security benefits results from inflation in our country. As inflation caused the price of necessities to rise, our citizens on fixed and limited incomes find they have less to buy the necessities of life. Therefore, I am favoring an increase in Social Security benefits which would provide for sliding scale increase in the future tied to the rising cost of living. The proposal which I am favoring also provides for an immediate 8 percent increase in Social Security payments. I believe that this is a sound approach to the problem and is not unreasonable as is the President's proposed 20 percent across the board increase."*

Even though he thought the Social Security program was established to help poor people too stupid to take care of themselves, he approved a modest increase and then raised that, in the wake of a flood of mail from the people back home.

"Pressure Mail"

Gardner's papers indicate that he didn't care much for the opinions of his constituents. At least not the opinions of average, working men and women who needed help with the various agencies of their government in Washington.

Three of the 23 boxes of Gardner's Congressional papers, now at the North Carolina Collection at the University of North Carolina at Chapel Hill, were labeled by his staff as "Pressure Mail." These files mostly contain correspondence from constituents inquiring and asking for help on a variety of routine matters dealing with the operation of government.

Letters from senior citizens asking their Congressman to support an increase in Social Security benefits are in the "Pressure Mail" file. So are hundreds of letters from constituents from the Fourth District asking Gardner to support federal legislation to improve education.

Letters from citizens telling him how they felt about the Vietnam War, highway safety, crime, firearms control and requests for information on applying for a job with the Post Office are all in the boxes which Gardner considered "Pressure Mail."

Vietnam War

The years that Gardner served in Washington were among the most critical during the entire Vietnam War. Lyndon Johnson had come to a tragic dead-end in his effort to end the war and announced that he wouldn't seek re-election. If ever the nation and the Congress needed strong leadership, it was in these trying and difficult years.

Gardner seemed to realize the significance of the problem.

On July 18, 1967, Gardner wrote Robert Wall, a constituent in Raleigh and said. *"The most pressing and controversial issue facing our nation today is the conflict in Vietnam.*

"Something must be done to bring this conflict to a quick and honorable conclusion for the security of the United States and the World.

"I am taking the liberty of sending a copy of a speech which I made in the House of Representatives on July 12, 1967, entitled "Vietnam Peace Proposal," in further response to your expressed interest in Vietnam."

Gardner's solution to the nation's most serious problem was to send a copy of a speech he'd made.

Civil Rights

Gardner served in Congress during some of the most racially turbulent years in the nation's history. Following the assassination of Rev. Martin Luther King, violence and riots spread across the nation.

In the wake of the King assassination, Congress passed a sweeping Civil Rights Bill which guaranteed minorities access to many rights and privileges already available to them under the Constitution but denied in practice. The Civil Rights Bill was passed largely along party lines with Democrats supporting it and Republicans voting against.

Gardner voted against the bill. He received so many letters asking him to explain his position that he wrote a form letter which his staff used to send to inquiring constituents. The form letter is among his papers on file in the North Carolina Collection. It reads:

"Dear XXXX: Thank you for your recent correspondence regarding the 1968 Civil Rights Bill.

"On April 10, the House completed action on the Administration backed Civil Rights Bill. By a roll-call vote of 250 to 172 the House accepted far-reaching Senate amendments which include open housing, anti-riot and gun control provisions, and an Indian rights section. The original bill, which the House passed last August, only provided for protection of persons exercising their civil rights by prescribing penalties for certain acts of violence or intimidations.

"I voted against this legislation for two basic reasons. The open housing provision will cover 80% of all housing sold or rented after 1969. I feel that one of the basic foundations of our

country and democracy has been our family life and our right of home ownership. I do not believe that it is the right of our Federal Government to tell one of our citizens to whom he must rent or sell his home. We simply cannot guarantee equality for everyone by taking away from one to give to the another."

Although the Civil Rights Bill of 1964 contained many provisions to which most Americans subscribe, Gardner focused his objection on the provisions which he knew would be inflammatory to many voters.

In October, 1967, Gardner issued his 43rd newspaper column to newspapers throughout the district. And in it, outlined what he considered to be the important work facing Congress. He cited important bills on social security, education, poverty, civil rights, copyright revision, tax surcharge, truth in lending, military pay and a raise for postal workers.

After stressing the scope and importance of the work that remained to be done, Gardner missed 56 percent of the roll call votes in the next year.

About the most that can be said about Gardner's service in Congress is that it was mercifully brief. Although he had begun his term with a bang, he concluded with a whimper, leaving a legacy of absenteeism that stands as one of the worst in the history of Congress.

VII

1968-1972
Twice Up, Twice Down

During his two years in Congress, Gardner introduced no legislation that had a remote chance of being passed. His constituency service was a classic case of ineptitude, and his fellow Republican in the House, Charles Jonas, had confided to friends in both parties that he was unimpressed with the young man from Rocky Mount.

Despite a record of service that would have caused many Congressmen to doubt their own chance of reelection, Gardner asserted that it was his record in Congress that qualified him to be Governor of North Carolina.

In the 1968 Republican gubernatorial primary, Gardner confronted Jack Stickley, a businessman with solid credentials in business, public service and the Republican party. What Stickley possessed in credentials, he lacked in charisma. He was neither youthful nor photogenic. The television camera seemed to baffle him.

Stickley, however, was supported by mainstream Republicans, including the highly regarded Congressman Jonas.

Stickley criticized Gardner's record in Congress, describing the youthful freshman Republican as a "Tuesday-to-Thursday Congressman." Gardner buried Stickley in the primary, one of the first in North Carolina for the Republican party.

While Gardner was polishing off Stickley, Bob Scott and J. Melville Broughton, Jr., sons of former Democratic governors, were waging a spirited contest for the Democratic nomination. Reginald Hawkins, a black candidate from Charlotte, also was in the Democratic primary contest for Governor. He was a wild card that made the contest uncertain.

Scott had served a term as Lieutenant Governor during Dan Moore's administration. He was clearly the front runner in the three-way contest. In the absence of Hawkins, Scott probably would have run away with the primary election.

National politics, the climate of civil turmoil in the nation and the escalating racial strife together had a profound impact on the 1968 elections in North Carolina.

In 1968, Lyndon Johnson, bogged down in Vietnam and beleaguered by critics for his handling of the war, declared that he would not be a candidate for reelection. Vice President Hubert Humphrey immediately declared that he would seek the Democratic nomination for President.

Robert Kennedy, senator from New York and brother of the slain John F. Kennedy, cast his hat into the Democratic ring seeking the presidential nomination. He was slain in Los Angeles, making it possible for Vice President Humphrey to win the nomination.

In 1968, Richard Nixon -- who had last been seen in public forums as the defeated candidate for Governor of California-- whining that the media "wouldn't have Nixon to kick around anymore"-- was seeking the Republican nomination for President as a "new Nixon."

George Wallace, Governor of Alabama, who briefly had stood in the schoolhouse door to protest desegregation before being moved aside by Federal marshals, was running for President as an Independent.

In April of 1968, Civil Rights leader, Nobel Peace Prize

winner and advocate of non-violence Dr. Martin Luther King was slain as he stood on a motel balcony in Tennessee.

In North Carolina, the candidates were hard at work on the campaign trails when news of the King assassination flashed across the news wires. Virtually all of them canceled campaigning and returned to their headquarters. Shortly thereafter, the major cities of the United States went up in flames, as blacks rioted in wild abandon, creating consternation throughout the land.

In North Carolina, curfews were clamped on cities and an eerie silence gripped urban streets at night. There was some sporadic violence, but nothing on the scale of the rioting that shook large cities such as Washington, D. C.

In the summer of 1968, the Democrats held their presidential convention in Chicago. A multitude of young people, calling themselves yippies, descended on the Windy City to confront Mayor Daly's police in a vague, but violent, protest against the Democratic party and the government. Daly's hard nosed cops used nightsticks and other weapons in an effort to remove the protesters from the city as they chanted, "The whole world is watching."

Politicians in North Carolina began talking tough about law and order. The phrase became code words designed to reassure whites that strong action would be taken against black rioters and demonstrators. The turmoil made it difficult for white candidates to appeal to black voters.

The civil discord and strife created the political climate in which Wallace could gain momentum. In North Carolina, Wallace's stance toward blacks, his record of resistance and his highly charged rhetoric directed at Washington, liberals and those he called "pointy-headed intellectuals," struck a responsive chord.

Gardner was torn. On the one hand, he had achieved political success as a symbol of the new Republicanism, youthful charismatic and hard-charging. However, many of Gardner's supporters were moving toward Wallace, and Gardner had to at least make overtures toward them.

But he could not do so without being disloyal to the Republican Party and to Richard Nixon in 1966. Nixon had come to Asheboro, the county seat of Randolph County, one of the staunchest Republican counties in North Carolina, and campaigned for Gardner in his successful battle against Harold Cooley. Gerald Ford, then the U.S. House Minority Leader, also came to the Fourth District to help Gardner. This made Gardner's flirtations with Wallace so much harder to bear for loyal Republicans.

During the 1968 campaign, jokesters delighted in saying that the youthful, gray-haired Gardner would go into a barbershop and tell the barber to trim his locks, add a bit of gray to the sides and a touch of red to his neck.

In order not to offend Wallace voters, Gardner began to state that he did not disagree with anything Wallace was saying in North Carolina. He also said that he supported Nixon, whose views on the issues of the time were far more moderate than those of Wallace.

Gardner was caught in a particularly difficult bind when Spiro Agnew came to North Carolina to campaign. As the Republican candidate for Governor, Gardner shared a Raleigh platform with Agnew as the Vice Presidential candidate criticized Wallace. Gardner tried to ignore the remarks.

Gardner headed the North Carolina delegation to the Republican National Convention in 1968, and had pledged to support Nixon. At the convention, Gardner refused to carry out his pledge. Instead he supported Ronald Reagan who, at that time, had not achieved the national stature which he would later acquire.

Many Republicans in North Carolina were angry at what they perceived to be Gardner's betrayal of the trust which the Republican Party had placed in him.

In 1968, Gardner was walking a political tightrope, seeking to make North Carolina voters believe that he was a friend of Wallace, Nixon and Reagan.

In 1992, Gardner again created concern among mainstream Republicans when he went to the beach on the Fourth of July rather than join President George Bush at a political event in the North Carolina community of Faith.

In the 1968 Democratic primary election, Bob Scott came in first, followed by Broughton, with Hawkins winning more than 100,000 mostly black votes. Broughton had achieved his primary goal of obtaining enough support to call for a runoff.

In the backrooms of the Broughton campaign organization the chances of winning in a runoff were debated. It was conceded that Scott, perceived to be more liberal than Broughton, would be the beneficiary of the Hawkins' vote.

The central issue confronting the Broughton campaign was whether it would be possible to succeed in a campaign in which, as one crass operative put it, "we will have to hang the black vote on Scott."

Broughton had no stomach for such a contest. As a member of the moderate-conservative wing of the party, he and his family had enjoyed cordial relations with black people for generations.

Moreover, Broughton was a supporter of predominantly black Shaw University and had frequently rendered legal advice to the institution. Broughton was not an aggressive advocate of social change, but he and most of the people around him were not racists. They valued their reputations as responsible citizens, able to work in harmony with black and white leaders.

Gardner had been counting on a rupture in Democratic ranks. He had hoped for a bitter runoff election between Scott and Broughton so that he could pick up votes from the losing side.

Broughton wanted to carry on his campaign -- if it could be done without resorting to polarizing racial politics. As a former chairman of the Democratic Party, he felt an obligation to act in the best interest of the party.

A phone call from Dan Moore, who had appointed him to the chairmanship of the Democratic Party, helped Broughton reach his decision. He decided against a runoff. He met with Scott before a packed room at the Sir Walter Hotel and declared his support for Scott and Democratic Party unity.

The period immediately following the primary elections was crucial. Democrats closed ranks, quickly dispelling any thought that Gardner might have had for capitalizing on division.

Mainstream Republicans such as Congressman Jonas and James Broyhill had campaigned hard for their friend, Jack Stickley. As leaders of the party before the Gardner political ascendancy, they had often played key roles in the selection of Republican candidates. Gardner's victory had relegated them to lesser roles in party affairs. It was reported that both Jonas and Broyhill "reluctantly" climbed aboard the Gardner bandwagon.

A number of Republicans were unhappy with the behavior

of Gardner in the primary. Trosper Combs, Republican candidate for Lieutenant Governor, blamed his loss of the nomination on Gardner. Combs said Gardner had handpicked Don Garren as the Republican candidate for Lieutenant Governor and had supported him in the primary.

Combs also charged Gardner with discouraging state Representative Jim Johnson from running for Lieutenant Governor by threatening to channel $250,000 into the campaign of his opponent. Combs charged that, with Gardner's nomination, "North Carolina Republicans have a one-man dynasty right now."

Johnson downplayed Combs' charges without actually denying them in a published newspaper report. The Associated Press reported that Gardner was "meeting with his campaign manager and could not be reached to comment on Combs' charges."

Shortly after the primary, Reginald Hawkins, the black candidate for the Democratic gubernatorial nomination, began to waffle on throwing his support to any candidate. In published reports, Hawkins stated that he thought Democrats had taken blacks for granted and that he was undecided as to whom to favor in the General Election.

Hawkins announced that he was considering throwing his support to Gardner, placing the young Republican candidate in a perplexing position. Gardner's stance was strictly anti-integration. He had expressed enthusiastic support for George Wallace. Many of his supporters were adamantly opposed to policies expanding civil rights and opportunities for blacks. Yet, Gardner knew that the sheer numbers of the black vote would be important -- perhaps crucial--in deciding the 1968 election.

How seriously he negotiated with Hawkins is not known. No one associated with the campaign--certainly not Gardner-- would comment. However, after a protracted period, Hawkins, in a lukewarm manner, endorsed Bob Scott. Gardner jumped on the issue. He charged that Scott had made some sinister deal with Hawkins to win black votes.

In short, Gardner sought to do what Melville Broughton, Jr., and even his most conservative supporters didn't have the stomach for -- he tried to "hang the black vote around Scott's neck." Scott got the great majority of the black vote, but

Gardner's heavy handed, racially charged statement backlashed against him. He was roundly criticized by the major media. The Charlotte Observer accused him of lying.

At the national level, the resurrected "new Nixon" was running strong against Humphrey, who had been battered by the civil strife surrounding the Democratic presidential convention, Humphrey reluctantly carried the Johnson record, an albatross he would have liked to discard, but could not. Johnson, seeking to claim a place in the history books for himself, was more interested in posturing as a statesman than in engaging in the political fray.

Democrats in North Carolina, many of whom did not agree with the Johnson policies of the past four years, were wary of the liberal Humphrey.

Gardner and the Republican Party were counting on a fractured Democratic Party being unable to hold together at either presidential or gubernatorial level in North Carolina. What they did not realize was that Hubert Humphrey and Statesville insurance man and political wheeler dealer Billy Webb, who had been the Democratic Party's national committeeman, had struck a strong personal friendship.

Webb, who was well connected to all branches of the Democratic Party in North Carolina, campaigned vigorously for Humphrey throughout North Carolina, winning over many Tar Heels to Humphrey.

As the presidential campaign progressed, Humphrey attracted traditional Democratic support groups and reached out with a cheerful aggressiveness that turned his contest against Nixon into a down-to-the-wire, neck and neck struggle.

Gardner's quandary deepened. Wallace was still running strong in North Carolina. Humphrey was gaining. Nixon did not appear to have the strength in North Carolina to help state and local Republicans.

Throughout eastern North Carolina -- the Wallace stronghold -- Gardner continued to link himself to Wallace positions. At one point Gardner, who had seized control of the Republican Party by presenting himself as the new Republican, said he would be as comfortable supporting George Wallace as he would be supporting Richard Nixon.

Congressman Jonas, who had supported Jack Stickley in the

North Carolina Republican primary and who had reluctantly supported Gardner after the primary, could stay silent no longer. He publicly criticized Gardner for a lack of party loyalty. Gardner refused to retract his tacit endorsement of Wallace. His actions left lingering doubt among many Republicans regarding his party loyalty.

In the wake of the civil and racial strife of 1968, Democrats and Republicans agreed that the general election was close. In the last crucial weeks of the campaign, Gardner began to falter.

Major newspapers in the State had begun to critically examine Gardner's record, his campaign tactics, the lack of substance in his proposals and the mean-spirit he conveyed.

In a major gaffe, the Gardner campaign sought large contributions by offering special treatment to the contributors--if Gardner were elected. Contributors who gave $1,000 or more were promised they would be included in a "Winners for Gardner Club." They would be issued coded stationery to use in corresponding with Gardner which would assure special attention.

The offer of special treatment for big contributors by a candidate for Governor was just the kind of issue that newspapers and broadcast stations loved. Scott capitalized on Gardner's blunder by telling voters that they only needed a regular postage stamp or a postal card to communicate with him.

To diffuse the issue, Gardner issued press releases and wrote letters to individuals. In his letter, Gardner sought to blame the gaffe on his organization. He wrote:

"Not long ago, you received a letter from W. E. Dansey asking that you join a "Winners for Gardner Club." That letter was sent out without my knowledge and, certainly without my approval. It is unfortunate that in all campaigns, certain people become over-zealous in their efforts to help the candidate."

Neither the press nor the public believed that the letter had been written and mailed without Gardner's knowledge or approval, and the issue dogged Gardner throughout the campaign.

Newspapers also reported that Gardner received more money from an ultra-conservative group established in 1964 than any other candidate in the nation. The amount of money actually given to Gardner was only $3,000, but the smell of it tainted

Gardner from the time it was disclosed until election eve.

As news coverage of Gardner's campaign became more intense and critical, Gardner turned peevish with the press. He had fancied himself a master of controlling news conferences and answering questions posed by reporters.

Under the harsh scrutiny of veteran political reporters, Gardner was less adept. He began to badger and bait the press. The scrutiny intensified. Gardner sought refuge by staging television news conferences which he felt presented him in a better light.

As the election approached, the contest between Gardner and Scott remained uncertain, but the momentum was clearly shifting. The Raleigh News and Observer, in a column by then-Associate Editor Tom Inman, speculated that Gardner was in trouble, had probably peaked, and would likely be defeated.

Gardner disagreed, but Inman's analysis proved to be accurate. As the returns poured in that November night in 1968, Gardner again experienced the bitter taste of defeat.

As he responded to the defeat, Gardner looked like the boxer he was once purported to be. Only this time, he looked not like a victorious gladiator, but more like a ring-weary contender who had caught a sucker punch in the mid-section.

Gardner tried to find solace in having come closer to victory than any Republican candidate for Governor in North Carolina in the 20th Century.

Democrats chortled, "Coming close only counts in horseshoes, not politics."

When Bob Scott handed Gardner his second political defeat in three elections, Gardner slunk away vowing that he was through with politics.

The 1972 Campaign

By 1972, Gardner had forgotten his vow of being through with politics and was hoping that the voters of North Carolina also had forgotten. Some had not.

Among these who had taken Gardner at his word was a young Boone attorney and State legislator, James Holshouser.

As a chairman of the North Carolina Republican Party and as a well-regarded legislator among Democrats and Republicans,

Holshouser had quietly begun to gear up for a race for the Governor's office. Holshouser was disconcerted and disappointed when Gardner beat him to the punch and filed for Governor in the 1972 Republican primary. However, he was not deterred. He also filed as a candidate in the Republican primary for Governor.

Gardner pooh-poohed his rival from the mountains of North Carolina. He sought to ignore him as much as possible. Instead, he directed his campaign rhetoric toward Democrats. Media reports suggested that Gardner felt that he would be a shoo-in for the nomination and that Holshouser would be easy to defeat. Apparently, Gardner overlooked a crucial statistic. Despite a strong campaign style and significant charisma on the campaign trail, Gardner had lost two-thirds of his campaigns up to that point. Holshouser presented a squeaky clean image. His rhetoric was low-key, sometimes lawyerly in its precision. Although initially he seemed overwhelmed by Gardner's rhetorical and campaign hyperbole, Holshouser quietly reminded people that he had never lost an election.

In the Democratic primary, a Greensboro millionaire businessman, Hargrove "Skipper" Bowles had squared off against Lieutenant Governor Pat Taylor of Wadesboro. With access to big bucks and a telegenic appearance, Bowles surged forward in the Democratic primary. AFL-CIO President, Wilbur Hobby of Durham and Reginald Hawkins, of Charlotte, were wild cards in the Democratic primary. Two other unknowns on the Republican side--Leroy Gibson of Jacksonville and Thomas Chappell of Greensboro--threw their hats into the GOP ring setting up potential run-offs on both sides.

The Republican primary appeared to be a classic case of the hare and the tortoise, with Gardner quickly outdistancing Holshouser.

In all of his previous campaigns, Gardner harassed his opponents, demanding public debates. In the 1972 campaign, he stonewalled Holshouser's request for debates, contending that he was more interested in debating a Democratic opponent, Pat Taylor.

Gardner campaigned, much as he always had--by touting his "business experience," promising that he would bring new efficiency to state government.

In his 1968 campaign for Governor, Gardner had virtually endorsed the third party presidential candidate, George Wallace. His betrayal of Nixon at the 1968 Republican Convention still rankled some Republicans.

Holshouser was too good a lawyer and too good a Republican to have forgotten Gardner's flip-flopping. At every occasion, he reminded Republicans of Gardner's flirtation with Wallace and of the injury this had inflicted on Republican party strength in North Carolina.

Gardner clearly was not a loyal Republican.

For example, Helen Godfrey of Goldsboro was the Wayne County Chairman of the Gardner for Governor Committee in 1968. In a letter to The News and Observer, she recalled that Gardner and his staff member ordered her to be sure that *"the word Republican was not to be seen in this office."*

Mrs. Godfrey noted that Gardner insisted that *"there was not to be any other candidate's campaign material, not even young Republicans' bookmatches"* in the office.

Gardner even went so far as to demand removal of a "Vote Republican" bumper sticker from a car that was participating in a political caravan in which Gardner was traveling.

Finally, said Mrs. Godfrey, she was told by Gardner's staff not to publicly divulge her support for Richard Nixon.

A former Cumberland County resident who had been active in Republican Party affairs and who asked not to be identified, described Gardner's interest in two-party politics thusly: "He's as interested in two party politics as a turkey buzzard is in philosophy. Jim Gardner is for Jim Gardner -- nothing and nobody else."

As the Republican campaign wore on, U. S. Congressman Charles Jonas, who early in Gardner's career had been singularly unimpressed with Gardner's congressional record, publicly declared his support for Holshouser. Gardner probably did not recognize the significance of the Jonas endorsement. It was a deliberate effort on the part of mainstream, old line Republicans such as Jonas and the Broyhills to move the fulcrum of Republican political leverage out of the east and back to the piedmont, the foothills and the mountains of North Carolina. It was successful.

Relying on earlier polls, Gardner and his organization

seemed oblivious to the steady advancement of Holshouser until it was too late.

On the night of Saturday, May 6, 1972, the race between Holshouser and Gardner was virtually dead even. Early Sunday morning, with 60 percent of the Republican vote in, Holshouser held a lead of not quite 2,000 votes.

The Cumberland County Republican, who does not want to be identified, was in Gardner's room that night. "Gardner looked like he had swallowed something that wouldn't go down, and he couldn't puke up," he said.

When all of the Republican votes had been counted, Gardner had edged ahead of Holshouser by a few hundred votes. The images of the two men contradicted the numbers. Gardner looked like a candidate defeated; Holshouser appeared triumphant. The two Republican unknown candidates had denied a majority to Gardner. Holshouser immediately declared that he would seek a runoff. Gardner looked stricken.

Gardner moved quickly to compound his political problems. He called a news conference to announce that the "White House," through a spokesman he refused to identify, had announced that a poll it had taken showed that Holshouser could not win the general election in North Carolina and that his candidacy would hurt Richard Nixon's chances of re-election against hapless Democratic candidate George McGovern. Gardner said the White House was urging Holshouser to withdraw.

Holshouser brushed off Gardner's statement, calling it a sign of "desperation." Holshouser was almost nonchalant in his dismissal of Gardner's assertion. He might have known that Harry Dent, highly regarded aide to President Nixon and a native of South Carolina with connections in North Carolina, was riding to his rescue. No sooner had Gardner made the assertion about the White House position than Dent came to Charlotte to say it was not true. Gardner had lied, according to Dent, and he had been caught.

North Carolina newspapers played the story big. Gardner became angry. He began to run against Holshouser and North Carolina newspapers. Earlier in the campaign, Gardner had written a letter to <u>The News and Observer</u> in Raleigh praising the paper for its even handed coverage of politics. The <u>N&O</u> said the paper received the letter as a "small but sincere overture of civility and appreciation."

During the second primary, Gardner, angry, desperate and somewhat befuddled, took on most of the major daily newspapers in North Carolina. He said that, if elected, he would attempt to change the First Amendment to the U. S. Constitution to restrict the press. Campaigning against the press is not a novel campaign tactic, observed the N&O. However, the paper stated that Gardner was taking on the press with "such unusual passion and public heartache that it seems only fair to reproduce his recent letter, and to relieve those readers who think him in genuine distress."

Again, Gardner was caught with egg on his face. Growing more desperate, Gardner reverted to his former pattern of baiting his opponent to debate. Holshouser, however, sensed that the tide had turned significantly in his favor. He ignored Gardner's pleas for debates, noting that Gardner had rejected eight different requests from him to debate in the first primary.

The night of the second Republican primary was a defining moment in the life of Jim Gardner. When the returns were finally counted, Holshouser, who began as the tortoise, had beaten Gardner, who had started as the hare.

It was close, to be sure. Holshouser, the boyish looking lawyer from Boone, had edged Gardner by slightly more than 1,500 votes.

Gardner proved to be neither gracious in defeat nor concerned about party unity. At first, he refused to concede victory to Holshouser. When he could not prevail in that position, Gardner had aide Earl Cox and others call a news conference to announce that Gardner's name would be entered as a third party candidate in the November general election. That was clearly a trial balloon and, when it did not float, Gardner packed it in, announced that he would support the two-party system in North Carolina and said he expected that other Republicans would do likewise. Gardner's statement was much less than a sportsmanlike concession to a man who had beaten him fairly and squarely.

At the outset of the campaign, Gardner had predicted that he would beat Holshouser with 70 percent of the vote. A young female Holshouser supporter put it this way: "Jim Gardner is sexy, but we beat him."

In the Democratic primary, Bowles trounced Pat Taylor in a runoff, and Nick Galifianakis beat Senator B. Everett Jordan, who had called for a runoff after Galifianakis had led in the first primary.

Bowles, arrogant in victory, declined to offer an olive branch of peace to Taylor and his supporters, unwittingly placing in jeopardy his expensive television-fueled victory. At the national level, McGovern, whom most Tar Heel Democrats could not stomach, won the presidential nomination. Jesse Helms easily won the Republican nomination for the U. S. Senate.

The 1972 general election proved to be a debacle for Democrats. Nixon, at the top of the ticket, crushed McGovern in North Carolina, sweeping in on broad coattails, Helms and other Republicans.

Holshouser stunned the state by defeating the well financed Bowles to become the first Republican elected to the North Carolina Governor's Office in the 20th Century.

Holshouser went on to establish a record of achievement-- acknowledged to be quite worthwhile by Democrats as well as Republicans.

Gardner again retreated from politics to begin a career as an entrepreneur which ended in financial disaster for himself and many who were associated with him.

VIII

Family Inns of America
Gardner's Business Empire Begins to Crumble

In the 1970s, Gardner's grandiose plans for a business empire collapsed under the weight of foreclosure, legal charges, often angry litigation, suspected corruption and general acrimony.

A cornerstone of Gardner's empire was to be Family Inns of America (FIA), a company formed to build and operate economy motels along the interstate highways.

The business failed, and as it was going under, FIA became the basis of a grand jury indictment of Gardner for securities violations, a civil action brought against him for fraud, negligence and mismanagement by a long-time associate and a suit for non-payment of legal fees by the very lawyer whose expertise and connections may have kept Gardner out of prison.

During the course of events surrounding the failure of FIA, Gardner's association with Joe Palumbo became public. Palumbo was later convicted of wrongdoing in a scheme designed to obtain money fraudulently from the Small Business Administration. And, Palumbo was alleged to have business dealings with a relative who had ties to organized crime.

Each chapter in the FIA affair provides troubling insight into the life and times of a man who contends that his business experience qualifies him to head a modern state.

Indicted

In March of 1976, Jim Gardner was indicted for securities fraud in connection with the sale of Family Inns of America stock to Thomas J. Head of Wilmington without having registered with North Carolina's Secretary of State as a dealer or salesman. Under North Carolina General Statutes, the offense is a felony.

On March 29, a New Hanover County Grand Jury determined there was enough evidence to return a true bill against Gardner and send the case to trial in Superior Court.

To defend against the charge, Republican Gardner retained the late Charlie Winberry, a prominent Democrat who practiced law in Gardner's hometown of Rocky Mount.

Winberry did for his client what many lawyers attempt to do. He sought out a judge whom he felt would be sympathetic to his client's position. Winberry was able to get the case scheduled before Judge Perry Martin, a member of former governors Kerr and Bob Scott's "Branch Head Boys," a group in which Winberry was a member in good standing.

Following the state's presentation of evidence, Winberry made a motion that the case against Gardner be dismissed not on grounds of innocence, but on the basis that the court didn't have jurisdiction in this matter. Motions for dismissal are seldom granted at the trial court level. Although most superior court judges hear the facts and let higher courts decide jurisdictional matters, Judge Martin, to the surprise of many, including the state's Attorney General, granted Winberry's motion and the securities charge was dropped.

Sued By Own Attorney

While the criminal case was settled, Gardner's problems with Family Inns were far from over. Attorney Winberry filed suit against his former client to collect his legal fees.

The complaint, still on file in the Nash County Courthouse alleges that as of August 1977, Gardner owed Winberry a total of $11,121.54 in unpaid legal expenses stemming from the securities fraud trial.

Winberry, in his claim against Gardner, noted that at no time during the proceeding had Gardner contested the billings which had been sent regularly along with proper documentation. He just didn't pay them.

Gardner didn't contest the charges at the time of the trial. He never responded to the summons to appear in court and a default judgment was entered against him for the full amount of the claim, plus interest and court costs.

Despite his frequent protestations, Gardner has not paid all his debts. By 1988, the debt to Winberry's law firm, with accrued interest had grown to more than $30,000. In October of 1988, Gardner settled the outstanding judgment with a promissory note for $15,000, agreeing to pay the successors to Winberry's law firm $5,000 each year until the entire amount was paid. One payment of $5,000 was made in the spring of 1989. No additional payment had been made on the debt as of July 1, 1992.

Longtime Friend and Ally Sues

The most revealing suit against Gardner was brought by his long-time associate and friend, David S. Wilson. Wilson was Gardner's aide during his single term in Congress and later joined Gardner as a business associate. Gardner thought so highly of his young protege that he praised Wilson for Wilson's contributions to a book, A Time To Speak published with Gardner's byline during his 1968 campaign for Governor.

Wilson joined Gardner in Family Inns of America and became financial vice president and treasurer of the company. Gardner, in legal papers, said Wilson directed the company's day-to-day activities.

During the early days of Family Inns of America, Wilson, like many others, was swept away by the prospect that the company would become successful, and he invested in the firm. In three different transactions over a period of 12 months from August 1972 through July of 1973, Wilson bought 29,000 shares of FIA stock for a total purchase price of $67,600.

Unlike many of the company's other investors, Wilson was not wealthy. He borrowed money to purchase the stock. The failure of the company not only left him without a job but also deeply in debt for the stock he had purchased.

After negotiating with Gardner for several months in the fall of 1973 and early spring of the following year for the return of his money, Wilson filed suit in U.S. District Court in Raleigh.

Named as defendants were James C. Gardner, JCG, Inc., a management company which Gardner owned; and Family Inns of America, Inc.

In a 25-page document, Wilson spelled out in graphic detail how the company operated, how it was financed, and why he thought it failed.

Allegations against his former friend and boss reflect poorly on Gardner's skill, business ethics and personal integrity. The suit contains, among other allegations, the following:

"Mismanagement.

"Plaintiff is informed and believes that Defendant Gardner's franchise arrangement was a sham proposal and a scheme to defraud FIA of its rights and properties under the Contracts of Lease.

"Defendant Gardner employed devices, schemes and artifices to defraud FIA and engaged in acts, practices and courses of business constituting frauds and deceits upon FIA.

"Discharged his duties not in good faith but in breach of his fiduciary obligations by causing FIA to act in transactions in which he had adverse interests in manners that were not just and reasonable to FIA.

"Caused FIA to perform at its expense obligations that were properly his or other real estate investors under the Contracts of Lease in construction of motels.

"Refused to enforce FIA's rights against Modular Corporation of America for breach of warranties in connection with the modular units used in construction of motels.

"Caused FIA to purchase motel signs of inferior design and quality from Timely Signs, Inc., another corporation in which he was a principal shareholder, caused FIA to pay Timely Signs, Inc., unjust and unreasonable sums and to assume its obligations, and refused to enforce FIA's rights against Timely Signs, Inc.

"Refused to enforce rights against suppliers of furniture and equipment for breach of warranties.

"Required FIA to incur unjust and unreasonable expenses

in repairing defective and inadequate construction in motels.

"Acted unfairly, unjustly and unreasonably in his own interest and not in the best interest of FIA in connection with proposed and purported franchising of motels owned by affiliated real estate investors as a result of prior corporate opportunities."

"Required FIA unjustly, unreasonably, and wrongfully to make advance rental payments to himself and JCG, Inc.

"Required FIA unjustly, unreasonably, and wrongly to make an advance rental payment to the Florence Family Inn Limited Partnership, because of an adverse interest.

"Schemed to pay from FIA's operating account an obligation not of FIA but of ELM Investments, Inc. for $50,000 and guaranteed by Defendants and schemed to omit disclosure....

"Defendant Gardner has mismanaged FIA, breached his fiduciary duties to it and has caused it to engage in transactions with him in which he had adverse interests and which were not approved by a majority of not less than two of the disinterested directors and which were not just and reasonable to FIA.

"In connection with the offer of sale and the sale to Plaintiff of 8,125 shares of FIA common stock on July 16, 1973, and by use of means or instrumentalities of interstate commerce and the mails, Defendant Gardner made an untrue statement of material fact and omitted to state a material fact necessary in order to make the statements made, in the light of circumstances under which they were made, not misleading, in that he falsely stated to Plaintiff that he, Defendant Gardner, had subscribed to and paid for 13,800 shares of FIA common stock for $17,000 and in that he failed to disclose to Plaintiff that he, Defendant Gardner, had or intended to cause his check in purported payment therefore to be held and not negotiated and that he, Defendant Gardner, did not intend to pay for the said shares."

In strong legal terms, stated over and over again, Wilson accused his longtime friend and former boss of mismanagement, fraud and a series of corporate transactions designed to transfer the wealth of a publicly-owned company into his own pockets.

Although Gardner denied each of the allegations which accused misconduct, he did offer Wilson an undisclosed incentive to drop the action, and the case was settled out of court.

The attorney for Wilson was Arch T. Allen III of Raleigh,

a prominent Republican who later served as Chairman of the Wake County Republican Party. Allen declined to talk about the case, or his current feelings toward Gardner.

While terms of the settlement between Wilson and Gardner were not disclosed, a document on file (Book 964 page 852) in the Nash County Courthouse may shed light on the matter. On August 2, 1974, Gardner assigned to Wilson one-half of his interest in the lease of a tract of property where a Family Inns of America franchise was located at Gold Rock. Nine months later, lending institutions foreclosed on that property for non-payment of loans.

David Wilson, contacted at the Virginia real estate firm where he works, refused to comment.

"I don't care to go into that again," he said politely.

In response to questions about what kind of Governor Gardner would make and if he were supporting his former associate, Wilson said, *"I haven't talked to him in a couple of years."*

IX

Other Business Ventures Go Belly Up

Carolando Corporation

Gardner's biggest flop was Carolando Center, a 248-acre development, near Orlando, Florida.

In a 1972 press conference in Raleigh, Gardner said, *"We believe Carolando Center will be a major dramatic occurrence even though it is being developed in an area of the United States where the dramatic is becoming commonplace."*

The facility was to include a 22-story, first-class hotel, motor inn, apartments, an office plaza, campground, 18-hole executive golf course, swimming pools, restaurants and a spectacular 650-foot tower that was to be the tallest in Florida. The tower, Gardner announced, would be so high that ultimately the Federal Aviation Authority would have to step in and decide its height so as not to threaten commercial aircraft. The complex was to be located near the main entrance of Disney World.

Exuberantly, Gardner predicted that Carolando Center would be the largest motor inn and hotel convention center in the world. There were other superlatives. Guests would be able to check into rooms without getting out of their cars through a drive-in check-in window.

Development of Carolando was announced as a joint venture between Carolando Corporation, Reynolds, Smith and Hills (RS&H), a Jacksonville, Florida architectural-engineering-planning firm and Cameron-Brown Investment Group (CBIG), a financial institution in Raleigh. CBIG was a real estate investment venture of Cameron-Brown, which was a subsidiary of First Union National Bank. CBIG had arranged nearly $20 million in loans for the project.

Gardner served as president, chairman of the board and was a major stockholder. By June of 1973, Carolando had lost more than two million dollars. It was delinquent on interest loan payments and unable to arrange new financing.

Gardner was forced out of the organization and it was dissolved. First Union National Bank was left holding a $20 million mortgage.

Cliff Cameron, now retired, was First Union's Chief Executive Officer at that time. He recalls the Carolando venture with some reluctance. Cameron was quite familiar with Cameron-Brown operations. He founded the company in Raleigh and built it into a successful lending institution before it was acquired by First Union, along with his services.

Cameron, who supported Gardner in his bid for Lieutenant Governor in 1988 but is not backing him for Governor in 1992, hesitates to place all of the blame for Carolando's failure upon Gardner.

"I don't know whether you can attribute the failure to poor management or rather the times," Cameron said, recalling that a lot of real estate ventures started during that period went sour. As Cameron remembers, First Union came out about even on the principal it loaned Gardner for the Carolando venture but had to carry the mortgage as a non-earning liability for some time.

But Marion Cowell has no doubts about whom to blame for Carolando's failure. Cowell is now senior vice president and general counsel of First Union Corporation. He dealt with several bad Gardner loans during the 70s when CBIG was a subsidiary.

"I can't believe that a man whose company has been

through bankruptcy and who has been sued, I don't know how many times, is actually qualified to be Governor of North Carolina," Cowell told the Durham Independent in the spring of 1992. "That just doesn't make sense to me."

First Union found a West Coast developer who acquired the property, completed the hotel portion of the plan and sold it a few years later. The vast entertainment complex laid out by Gardner during the 1972 press conference was never built.

Peter Ploss who worked with Gardner at Carolando, is not kind in his recollections.

"Jim Gardner is a snake oil salesman," Ploss said. "He is a good salesman but a poor manager. He doesn't follow through on details."

Ploss said that Gardner was forced out of the Carolando venture when it became evident he couldn't handle a large, complex business.

Brandywine Bay

About the same time Gardner started the huge resort development in Orlando, Florida, he began an upscale 1,100-acre residential community near Morehead City in Carteret County called Brandywine Bay. Plans called for 46 condominium units and some 600 individual homes built around a scenic golf course.

Long before the ambitious plans became a reality, Gardner was forced out when CBIG foreclosed on the property because he had failed to make payments on $9 million in outstanding loans.

In addition, to defaulting on the CBIG loans, Brandywine Bay also failed to pay numerous suppliers and contractors hundreds of thousands of dollars, resulting in the filing of a number of liens and judgments in the Carteret County Courthouse.

Although CBIG took a heavy loss from Gardner's bad investments, an erie camaraderie existed between Gardner and CBIG officers.

CBIG president and managing trustee W. J. Smith, Jr. told news media at the time foreclosure proceedings were begun, "Brandywine and CBIG have simply reacted in an adverse financial situation which has been reported previously."

CBIG found a buyer who completed the project. Today Brandywine Bay appears to be a successful development, but there is no mention of Gardner in the promotional literature of Brandywine Bay. A property salesperson when asked about the resort's history replied, "I think it was started by some politician from Raleigh who went bankrupt or got in some kind of trouble and was put out." She didn't know that the resort's founder was the state's Lieutenant Governor.

Modular Corporation of America

Though Gardner says he has never filed for bankruptcy protection, one of the companies he helped start ended up in bankruptcy court in 1974 with his "fingerprints" all over the company's troubled financial operations.

Modular Corporation of America (MCA) was formed in August of 1971 to produce modular units for motels and apartment projects. A major customer of MCA was to be Family Inns of America.

Principal investors with Gardner in Modular Corporation were Greensboro real estate developer Harold Wenal, and Gastonia businessman and North Carolina Senator Marshall Rauch. Over the years, Rauch became one of the Senate's most respected and influential members.

Although Gardner said during bankruptcy proceedings that he was only a passive stockholder and played no active role in the day-to-day affairs of Modular Corporation, bankruptcy records revealed that he was paid $52,500 in 1973 by the company for serving as vice president and a director. In that year, according to bankruptcy records, Gardner was the company's highest paid officer. Yet, he told a Charlotte newspaper reporter less than a year later that he didn't remember serving as an officer of Modular Corporation.

In mid-1972, the company reported a pretax profit of $150,000 and the future was bright. Modular Corporation had an important decision to make, as Wenal explained to a Charlotte business writer:

"The company had to make up its mind and decide whether it wanted to remain a small entity, with $1,000,000 to $1,500,000 a year in sales and $200,000 to $250,000 a year in profits, or whether it wanted to expand," Wenal said.

Gardner and Wenal decided to shoot the moon. Rauch

decided to sell. He sold his entire interest in Modular Corporation back to the company for the same amount of his original investment, $33,000. He also resigned all positions with MCA and attempted to break all ties with the company and its remaining principals.

In addition to manufacturing modular motel units which had been selling briskly, the company began manufacturing modular units for apartment complexes. That decision proved to be fiscally fatal. A new production facility in Charlotte took most of the company's capital and bills started piling up. Soon, the company was some $400,000 short of funds needed to pay its debts. Gardner and Wenal attempted to sell their interest in late 1973.

A buyer was found through Jim Gardner's contacts in Family Inns of America and on December 10, 1973 Modular Corporation was sold under highly favorable terms to an Atlanta outfit called Intervest.

Intervest paid nothing down for Modular Corporation, which had about $100,000 in its bank accounts at the time of the transaction, but promised to pay $2 million in three to five years.

An initial payment of $165,000 was due January 31. But even before that date, Intervest checks to MCA began to bounce. Wenal and Gardner had the sale nullified and resumed ownership. By that time, Modular Corporation's bank accounts had been emptied.

Then Wenal and Gardner discovered that the three owners of Intervest had all been convicted in Federal District Court in Atlanta the previous summer of fraud, interstate transportation of stolen property, mail fraud, and conspiracy. The convicted swindlers were Ralph V. Thomas, Paul L. Wayman and Glenn Bryan Smith. All three are mentioned in a book by Jonathan Kwitny entitled, The Fountain Pen Conspiracy, a book about professional swindlers.

At the time they agreed to buy Modular Corporation, Intervest's owners each faced prison sentences of three to five years. They were out of jail on appeal bonds. Following a bond hearing in February of 1974, at which Wenal and others testified, their bonds were revoked.

Immediately after this turn of events, Gardner and Wenal began bankruptcy proceedings for Modular Corporation.

In the bankruptcy filing, the company listed assets at $200,000 and liabilities at $1.6 million. Among its creditors were a list of some 250 firms and individuals, mostly small businesses scattered throughout Piedmont North Carolina.

Also among the company's creditors were the IRS and the North Carolina Department of Revenue, which were owed more than $150,000. Court documents also show that Gardner was paid his $52,500 salary and bonus in May of 1973, the same month the company stopped paying its taxes to the state of North Carolina and to the IRS. But two months after it stopped paying taxes, the company bought an airplane for $60,000.

When the fiscal wreckage of Modular Corporation was put to rest in bankruptcy court, there remained a $750,000 note, held by First Union Bank, for which the three principal investors had pledged their personal security in addition to the company's assets.

During one of the numerous court appearances amid the bankruptcy proceedings, Wenal mentioned to one of the principals that he was going to the bathroom. He left and did not return. Federal officers couldn't find the once high-profile entrepreneur anywhere in the South. Acquaintances say he has emerged back in the real estate business in Florida.

Gardner, on the advice of his attorney, disavowed any responsibility for the loss. That left Marshall Rauch as the only financially responsible member of the trio available for litigation.

When First Union National Bank sought repayment, Wenal had fled, and Gardner appeared to lack sufficient assets which could be seized to satisfy the debt. Only Rauch, who had been gone from the company for several months was considered by First Union as a worthy target. Although Rauch had sold his interest in the company months earlier, the bank sued him for the entire debt which had grown to nearly $2 million. He was advised by both his attorney and accountant to file personal bankruptcy in order to avoid paying off the liability which should have been shared equally with Gardner and Wenal. Rauch refused.

At great personal sacrifice, Rauch raised the money by mortgaging his home, selling property and borrowing against a successful business. He paid the entire debt.

When confronted with the pending First Union claim, Gardner said that on the advice of his attorney he was not obligated, and he didn't pay a dime. Harold Wenal continued to evade the court.

Jim Gardner: Minority Entrepreneur?

The record of another Gardner scheme is preserved in the proceedings of a committee of the United States House of Representatives which looked into a widespread scandal of the Small Business Administration.

The Small Business Administration was the favorite trough where well-heeled Republicans found favor during the early 70s. Under the guise of helping struggling small businesses, the SBA poured millions of dollars into ventures that were later the subject of congressional investigations and criminal prosecutions.

One such venture was the Virginia Waffle Shoppes, a North Carolina company started by Gardner. Although he planned to build the waffle shop restaurants in North Carolina, Gardner sought funding through the SBA office in Richmond, Virginia. This was in violation of SBA policy.

His associate in this venture was Joe Palumbo, a Charlottesville businessman whose sister was romantically linked to Tom Regan, head of the Richmond SBA office.

Gardner's application for a $200,000 SBA loan was approved; however, before it was funded, both Palumbo and Regan were indicted for a major fraud scheme, convicted and sentenced to prison.

Gardner escaped prosecution because he had not received any government funds. However, his SBA application raised the eyebrows of several members of Congress with whom he had served.

Among the questions they raised about Gardner: Why did he file for the SBA loan in Virginia rather than North Carolina, in violation of SBA rules? Did he file as a minority entrepreneur, as indicated by a prominent congressman?

The matter was investigated by two different congressional committees which spent weeks probing through numerous attempts, many of them successful in ripping off the SBA. Gardner's Waffle Shoppes loan figured prominently in two days of hearings in October of 1973 and for three days each in November and

December of 1973.

At first Representative Parren Mitchell of Maryland outlined the Gardner scheme in October in a hypothetical scenario:

"Let's assume, hypothetically, that there was a candidate, a Republican, who ran for Governor in one of the Southern States. He was not successful in his quest for the Governor's office. He was a businessman in his own right and like every good businessman, he wanted to expand his business. He looked at the 8(a) set-aside programs and other programs. So he found himself three rather naive black folks. He said, 'look, I want you men to come into my company and I will put up the money for you. Here is $20,000 for you and $20,000 for you.'

"...These men buy in their stock--he gives it to them really. They have no voice, no participation, no understanding of that business. They are really silent, muted partners existing in name only. Then this same unsuccessful candidate for Governor, Republican, white, in one of our Southern States, would come in and say, 'I want an 8(a) contract, and I have a fully integrated business. We are disadvantaged. We meet all of the criteria.' How do you act against this? In short, what I am getting at, the danger of a highly politicized kind of thing occurring in both OMBE and SBA. How would you guard against that kind of case."

A month later, Rep. Mitchell referred back to this case, and at that time indicated that the details hadn't really been hypothetical.

"Let's start with James Gardner, the unsuccessful Republican candidate for Governor of North Carolina who formed a company called Virginia Waffle Shoppes," Rep. Mitchell said.

"I have a particular interest in that case because when the officials of SBA were before another subcommittee on which I serve, I presented this case...as a hypothetical case, although I had full knowledge it was not hypothetical."

We asked Gardner if he had made application for a SBA loan as a minority. He declined to respond.

We also asked Gardner about his associate, Joe Palumbo, who was convicted of numerous counts of fraud in the Richmond SBA scandal and sentenced to five years in prison. Again, Gardner declined to answer.

Gardner and Palumbo were associates in the Virginia

Waffle Shoppes venture. Had the company become successful, one of Palumbo's numerous subsidiaries would have provided equipment for the Waffle Shoppes.

Joining Gardner and Palumbo in pledging to repay the SBA loan were Sherman Kennedy and William B. Brown. SBA's credit reports on Kennedy listed 23 bank overdrafts, three collections and five judgments. Against Brown there was one suit and two judgments.

The SBA investigation file also revealed some contradictory information about Gardner's financial status at the time he asked for the SBA loan. According to information Gardner provided to the SBA, on the loan application dated May 28, 1973, he stated his net worth was more than $4 million and that he had assets totaling nearly $9 million, and that his wife's assets were worth more than $100 million.

If those statements had been true Gardner would not have been eligible for a SBA loan in the first place.

Palumbo's net worth was listed as more than $1 million.

The congressional hearings also turned up an intriguing connection between Palumbo and a relative, Samuel Calabrese, who had been exposed for developing a scheme on the West Coast to defraud the SBA through multiple loan guarantees.

Forced out of business on the West Coast, Calabrese set up an operation, with Palumbo as the front man, through the Richmond SBA office.

Palumbo submitted numerous loan applications totalling some $11 million for a variety of businesses which failed, leaving the taxpayers burdened with the responsibility of paying off the loans. In addition to Palumbo, both Regan and Calabrese were convicted of fraud. During both the prosecution of Calabrese and during the congressional hearings into the matter, Calabrese's name was linked to organized crime.

Another Lawsuit

In 1971, Gardner entered into an agreement with Parker's Barbecue to operate a restaurant, using the established Parker's name. The agreement specified that Gardner was to pay a franchise fee to the owners for use of the name.

The agreement seemed to be satisfactory to everyone until

May, 1982, when Parker's sued Gardner

Court documents filed by Parker's Barbecue in Superior Court in Wilson County claim that Gardner stopped making the franchise payments and began running advertising suggesting that Parker's Barbecue had become Gardner's Barbecue.

In addition to failing to pay a franchise fee totaling $14,639.71, Parker's accused Gardner of using paid advertising on the radio and on billboards to say that "Parker's Barbecue is now Gardner's . . . and to communicate to the general public and the patrons of Parker's that Gardner's has in effect absorbed Parker's and that Parker's no longer exists but is in some fashion merged into Gardner's."

That was not true, Parker's Barbecue maintained.

The matter was settled out of court in September of 1983. Although terms of the settlement were not disclosed, Gardner stopped using the Parker's name.

The Parkers would not discuss the case.

"We're in business," said Henry Parker. "And we don't want to say anything adverse about a politician."

Gardner vs. His Employees

Some large institutions and many wealthy individuals lost money in Gardner's business deals. However, the losses of wealthy individuals and institutions, although quite large, were not as personally painful as losses suffered by some working men and women, dependent on salaries.

Norma Jean Burnley and David Hendricks were employed by a Gardner-owned Fosdick's Seafood Restaurant. Burnley was employed by Gardner October 22, 1985, as a waitress for a weekly salary of $270. Hendricks was paid $350 per week.

At the time the action was filed against Gardner on April 20, 1987, the two employees charged they had been underpaid a total of more than $15,000 for overtime they worked.

The specific amount as stated in the claim was $3,978.75 for Burnley and $12,134.07 for Hendricks. A jury trial was requested in the U.S. District Court for the Eastern District of North Carolina Raleigh Division.

The matter dragged on for more than a year.

Before the case came to court, Gardner tried to get a

postponement. He said he had retained a lawyer not fully familiar with the case who also was scheduled to be in court in Western North Carolina on another case.

Gardner also argued that his "fulltime duties as a political candidate for state-wide office severely limited the time and attention he can devote to this matter until after the general election."

U. S. District Judge Earl Britt denied the request for delay and ordered the trial to begin immediately.

Gardner's company avoided the potentially embarrassing trial by agreeing to pay the plaintiffs a total of $7,000. In addition, the company was ordered to pay $8,346 in attorney fees and an additional $1,468 in court costs.

One Case Not Settled

Most of the legal cases against Gardner have been settled one way or the other. Many of the judgments expired after the 10-year statutory period, unrenewed and unpaid. But one case remained outstanding as of July, 1992.

According to a complaint filed in Wake Superior Court, Sal and Peggy Montalbano assert that Gardner's Barbecue, Inc., breached their contract to sublease a building in Raleigh on which the barbecue restaurant was the leaseholder of record.

The Montalbanos said they subleased the building after negotiations with Gardner and the late Ben Robinson, a Gardner's Barbecue employee. Under terms of the sublease, the Montalbanos agreed to repair and renovate the building and Gardner's Barbecue was to reimburse them for their expenditures.

The sublease terms also specified that during the summer months when N.C. State University attendance was low, Gardner's would accept a promissory note in lieu of the rent. Gardner's agreed to pay the rent on the building to the owners of the property, Avent Ferry Associates, Ltd.

The Montalbanos contend that while they were renovating the building and installing nearly $65,000 worth of restaurant equipment, Gardner failed to make rent payments to the owners, as required by terms of Gardner's original lease and the Montalbanos' sublease.

Shortly after opening a restaurant in the building, known as the Brass Lantern, the Montalbanos discovered that Gardner had failed to keep up his rent payments.

Owners of the building took possession of the recently renovated building and the newly installed restaurant equipment, putting the Montalbanos out of business.

The Montalbanos were forced to vacate the building and abandon their restaurant business. Shortly thereafter, however, the Montalbanos learned that Gardner had caught up the rent payments and had established a Gardner's Barbecue Restaurant in the building. Gardner removed the $65,000 worth of restaurant equipment installed by the Montalbanos and still has not returned it, they say.

Montalbano believes that, from the outset, Gardner intended to break the contract and obtain renovation of the building which he had been unable to complete because of his own financial instability.

In the spring of 1992, Montalbano suffered a mental breakdown, brought on, he said, by the financial loss he suffered in his dealings with Gardner.

"That investment was all I had in the world," Montalbano said. *"In fact, I had to borrow to raise part of the money and I'm still paying off the loan at $575 a month.*

"Jim Gardner is a very unethical man. No, I wouldn't trust him again. I certainly won't vote for him for Governor. I'm a Republican but I will vote Democratic this year."

Montalbano added that he first met Gardner during his campaign for Governor in 1972. *"I supported him then. In fact, I worked in his campaign. He didn't remember, but I did."*

X

1988,
New Version
of Old Gardner

In 1988, to the astonishment of both Republicans and Democrats, Gardner returned from political limbo to win his party's nomination for Lieutenant Governor and in the general election to defeat the Democratic nominee, Tony Rand.

Gardner had aged since voters had last seen him. He appeared to be a kinder, gentler version of his earlier self. However, his campaign against Rand raised the level of political acrimony several notches and resulted in his opponent's bringing an unprecedented suit for libel. Like many of his other ventures, Gardner's campaign for Lieutenant Governor resulted in litigation.

When the 1988 elections began to take shape in North Carolina, Gardner was a footnote in Tar Heel politics. Those younger voters who knew him at all were only vaguely aware of his early and brief role in the Hardee's Restaurant chain. Many older voters of both parties who had followed his failed careers in politics and business considered him to be a political pariah, unfit for almost any role in the public life of the State.

Jack Hawke, master political manipulator, saw in his old friend something many others did not see. Perhaps what Hawke saw were the smoldering embers of the political fire that had raged in Gardner's belly a generation earlier. Possibly, he saw the remnants of a political ego that, through proper nurturing, could be restored sufficiently to serve as the catalyst that would propel Gardner forward as a socially acceptable candidate.

Despite its growth, the Republican Party in 1988 did not have a deep bench of candidates from which a strong team could be fielded. If not Gardner, who? That was a paramount question in the backrooms of the Republican Party. With Governor Jim Martin's popularity strong and his chances of re-election good, Hawke and other Republican strategists felt that Gardner, properly handled and presented to the public, could complement Martin's candidacy.

From the outset, Gardner presented himself as a strong helpmate to Martin. At every opportunity, he praised Martin's record, which at that time consisted principally of four years of confrontation with the Democratically controlled General Assembly. Martin's telegenic features and his low-keyed manner of dealing with political issues combined to produce a political persona that many North Carolinians of both parties found quite acceptable. However, he had lost many confrontations with the Legislature and his record of achievement was scarce.

Democrats -- especially Ken Eudy, Executive Director of the State Democratic Party -- delighted in referring to Martin as North Carolina's _sitting_ governor, with emphasis on the word sitting.

When the Republican and Democratic primaries were over, Martin and Gardner were pitted against Bob Jordan, the incumbent Lieutenant Governor and Tony Rand, a senior member of the North Carolina Senate. From the outset, Martin led Jordan in the polls. However, Rand got off to an early, strong start against Gardner and seemed headed for an easy victory.

The Rand campaign ran ads questioning Gardner's judgment in his string of failed business ventures and calling attention to Gardner's record of absenteeism as a U. S. Congressman.

Hawke describes the Rand ads as good ads "as far as

Rand's campaign was concerned." He also contends that the Gardner campaign felt that Rand's ads opened the door to the retaliatory ads which were developed and used against the Cumberland County Democrat.

"We could not have won the campaign without the perception that was developed about Tony," recalls Hawke. "Gardner was hurt by the absentee ads and hurt more by the judgment ads. We even got behind in the polls for a while."

Hawke and Gardner fired a volley of ads charging Rand, a lawyer, essentially with being an accomplice to a drug dealer Rand had represented in a legal matter a decade earlier.

Gardner carefully withheld the negative attack ads until the closing days of the campaign, then spent one-third of his total campaign media budget to air charges which so infuriated Rand that he filed a lawsuit charging Gardner with libel.

Rand, is a Wake County native with political connections in Raleigh and legal connections throughout the State.

"The SOB lied about everything," says Rand of Gardner. "I felt like I had to sue him, and I'm glad I did."

In a deposition given during the pre-trial maneuverings, Gardner contended that he knew nothing about the ads. To dozens of questions seeking to determine Gardner's participation in the preparation and airing of the ads, Gardner would say, "I don't know." That phrase became a standard reply throughout the lengthy questioning by attorneys.

Although he later swore he knew nothing about the content or origin of the ads, Gardner, immediately following the filing of Rand's suit, challenged Rand to debate him publicly on the merits of the allegations contained in the Gardner ads. Haranguing opponents to debate is one of Gardner's standard campaign tactics.

Rand's suit against Gardner appeared to be headed for a precedent-setting jury trial that could have forever altered the tenor and tone of political campaigns in North Carolina when it was abruptly settled -- out of court.

Included in the settlement was a public apology by Gardner to Rand. Ask Rand how much money changed hands and he simply folds his arms and smiles like a Cheshire cat.

"Our agreement prohibits me from commenting on the financial terms of the settlement," he says. Then he chuckles with satisfaction. Rand's body language and his attitude indicate that he got a large measure of satisfaction from his political foe.

Although Gardner did not explain the basis for it, he filed a countersuit against Rand after Rand had sued him.

With all the ammunition he had against Gardner, many people wondered why Rand settled out of court.

"I'm not a wealthy man," says Rand. "Going into a protracted suit in the courtroom costs a lot of money, and there is never a guarantee as to how a case will be settled. The out-of-court settlement with Gardner satisfied those objectives which I might have achieved at trial."

Was money paid by Gardner to settle the suit? Was it adequate for the damage? Neither Rand nor Gardner will comment. In his few comments about the case, Gardner has sought to minimize his involvement and whatever payment he might have made to settle it. Rand just smiles.

Suits for libel by politicians are rare. A suit by one candidate charging libel by another is even rarer.

In lengthy depositions, given by Gardner and Herman E. Gaskins, Jr. of Washington, North Carolina, to H. Gerald Beaver and Harold E. Carlin, the background for the bizarre litigation is provided in detail.

Following is a summary of the case as revealed in those depositions:

From July 4, 1976, until late October, 1978, Gaskins was an assistant United States Attorney for the Eastern District of North Carolina.

He had been a law clerk for Judge John Larkins of the United States District Court, Eastern District of North Carolina, for 11 months prior to being appointed assistant U. S. Attorney. Prior to that he had been a law student at the University of North Carolina at Chapel Hill.

Gaskins was hired by Thomas McNamara, the U. S. Attorney at that time, and was retained by McNamara's successor, George Anderson, who was appointed by the Carter Administration. McNamara was a Republican, Anderson a Democrat.

When Gaskins was hired, the U. S. Attorney's office was staffed primarily with Republicans and a few Democrats. The political complexion changed when Anderson was appointed. Although there were no wholesale firings, a transition was effected which resulted in a greater number of Democrats being named and fewer Republicans.

After about three months with the civil section of the U. S. Attorney's office, Gaskins was moved to the criminal section. In that position, he had responsibility for the prosecution of all criminal cases in the Elizabeth City, New Bern and Wilmington divisions.

Sometime in 1978, Gaskins became responsible for prosecuting three large marijuana smuggling cases that were pending in the Eastern District.

At that time, there was a turf battle going on between the U. S. Customs Agency and the U. S. Attorney's office. Jack Dolan, now deceased, was the customs agent who was to play a larger role in this matter.

On December 9, 1977, George Purvis, Jr. and other men by the names of Lampros, Phillips, Grant, Platshorn and Meinster were the targets of a drug bust on the Cape Fear River at Wilmington.

A boat loaded with marijuana was seized on the Cape Fear River and one man, Lee Smith, was arrested.

Purvis, although the focus of much investigative attention, was not arrested, nor were any indictments outstanding against him.

Shortly after the arrest of Lee Smith, Purvis contacted Rand to discuss his potential legal problems and mentioned to Rand that he had left some of his belongings at the Hilton Hotel in Wilmington. Following his conversation with Purvis, Rand called Gaskins, informed him that he was representing Purvis and suggested that Gaskins might want to talk with Purvis.

Gaskins contends that he does not remember the telephone call from Rand.

Following his conversation with Purvis, Rand asked a Wilmington lawyer, James Nelson, to go to the Hilton, pay the hotel bill and collect the personal property there which belonged to Purvis.

Nelson did that. He took possession of $76.09 in cash, a pair of socks, a pack of cigarettes, a pair of shoes, a dart gun, and a citizens band radio receiver. No illegal substances were found in the room.

Attorney Nelson took the items home with him and the DEA and customs officials later requested that they be turned over to them.

Rand suggested that the officers provide a subpoena or some document that would protect the lawyers from client claims for releasing documents that belonged to the client. No subpoena was issued.

Sometime after the interdiction of the drugs, Purvis went to Tony Rand's apartment to see him. Rand was not there. Purvis called Rand and told him he thought he was in trouble and might be arrested.

Rand advised Purvis to call Dolan, the customs agent, and turn himself in, and that he (Rand) would represent him if the matter came to trial. Purvis visited Rand's apartment on Friday. Rand had to be away for the weekend. When Rand was informed that Purvis could not reach Dolan, Rand told him to keep trying and stay at the apartment; they would get together on Monday when Rand got back into town and arrange for Purvis to turn himself in.

Over the weekend, Purvis left Rand's apartment, went to Raleigh-Durham airport and flew to Miami, Florida. He surrendered to Federal authorities in Florida and became a cooperating witness for the government.

On the basis of these events, Gaskins said he wanted to prosecute Rand as an accessory after the fact of a felony because Rand had the items from the hotel room removed.

A decade later, these events became the basis for a series of newspaper ads, and radio and television commercials which were used by Jim Gardner in his successful campaign against Tony Rand for the office of Lt. Governor.

Gaskins contends that he never met Gardner, never worked for him, played no role in the Gardner campaigns. He contends that he became upset about news articles and editorials describing Rand's efforts to expand grand jury roles in the prosecution of drug offenses.

On his own, says Gaskins, he contacted Jack Hawke and met with him and Robert Jones, an employee of the Republican

Party, and together they drafted a statement alleging that Rand was guilty of inconsistent behavior and implying that he was guilty of a felony and the target of an investigation.

The statement was delivered by Gaskins with the help of the Republican Party at a news conference in front of the Federal Building in Raleigh. The press dealt harshly with Gaskins and did not exploit the accusations to the satisfaction of the Republican Party.

Jones, Hawke and others associated with the Republican Party and the Gardner campaign fashioned a number of radio and television commercials which accused Rand of being in cahoots with drug smugglers, with providing them with a hideout, with helping them to escape authorities, with removing evidence from a hotel room.

Incidentally, Gaskins, as a lawyer, has represented many drug dealers, and concedes that Rand's behavior regarding George Purvis was not unusual.

The Gardner ads accused Rand of providing clothing for Purvis to wear, although the difference in size between Rand and Purvis would have made Purvis appear ridiculous in Rand's clothes. This information was provided by a female topless dancer named Margaret or Mandy O'Banion, according to the deposition.

Following the filing of the suit by Rand charging Gardner with libel, Gardner was interviewed at length about his knowledge of the ads and the reasons why they were run during the closing days of the campaign. He professed to the end that he knew nothing. Gardner let Jack Hawke, his daughter Terry Noble, Robert Jones, his advertising agency and others take the heat for the ads which became the basis for a rare libel suit based on political campaign tactics.

XI

Gardner In The Crystal Ball
What Kind of Governor Would He Be?

Three truths are self-evident: Leopards don't change their spots; zebras don't change their stripes; and old politicians don't change their ways in the sunset of their careers.

As one considers the kind of Governor Jim Gardner might be, one should keep foremost in mind those truths. Historians know that the past is prologue to the future, and, thus, the way ahead is lighted by the actions and activities of the past.

Despite dozens of television commercials, perhaps hundreds of public appearances, numerous news conferences, a long and litigious business career and two terms in public office, Gardner remains something of an enigma. His answers to questions posed by reporters and others who would seek to understand him appear, superficially, to be candid. Closer examination almost invariably reveals that Gardner always speaks in self-serving terms.

Gardner's record in business and politics contains the most important truths about this man who would be Governor: He always promises more than he delivers. He always claims more credit for successes than he deserves. When things go wrong he always seeks to avoid responsibility and to place the blame elsewhere. When he feels the need to do so, he fabricates facts, dissembles and distorts the truth.

Unless Gardner can accomplish what leopards and zebras cannot and what old politicians will not, he will bring those characteristics that have remained with him over the decades to the Governor's office, should he be elected.

His term as Lieutenant Governor, 1989-1992, provides the most recent record by which one might judge Gardner's actions as Governor.

When Gardner was running for the office of Lieutenant Governor, he promised to be a helpmate to Governor Martin, a strong right arm for Martin's proposals in the court of public opinion. The record indicates he did not deliver on his promise.

When Martin needed Gardner to help build public support for programs which Martin felt were needed Gardner left his Governor twisting slowly in the wind while he sought political refuge through passive opposition.

The office of Lieutenant Governor in North Carolina has always been a matter of concern to governmental scholars. Constitutionally, the Lieutenant Governor is a member of the executive branch of government. In practice, however, the Lieutenant Governor traditionally has played a leading role in the legislative process.

Gardner's election as Lieutenant Governor would have given the Republican Administration a much stronger hand in legislative matters--if the old rules had been maintained. Gardner's campaign promises to help Governor Martin deal with the Legislature was a clarion call to action by leading Democrats in the North Carolina General Assembly.

In order to maintain legislative independence, the North Carolina Senate felt compelled to balance the scales between the legislative and executive branches of government. The most effective means to that end was to neuter the new Republican Lieutenant Governor.

In one of the first acts of the 1989 Session, the North Carolina Senate stripped Gardner of all the traditional powers of the office, leaving him only two tasks: presiding over the Senate, a largely ceremonial chore, and serving as a member of the North Carolina Board of Education which meets once a month.

Gardner was left with very little to do, a staff of 12 people and a budget of $600,000 to help him do it. North Carolina's constitution provides that the Lieutenant Governor can undertake any constitutionally approved executive tasks assigned to him by the Governor.

In late May of 1992, after nearly four years of Gardner's stewardship, Governor Martin was asked by the authors in a special written request to identify the achievements of Gardner as well as Gardner's special strength of character and the overall political vision which Martin feels qualify the Lieutenant Governor to succeed him as Governor of North Carolina. Martin's response was silence.

Although Martin had authority to assign Gardner many tasks and responsibilities, he chose to give him only two assignments of any real potential--the chairmanship of something called the Drug Cabinet and chairmanship of the Western North Carolina Environmental Council.

Less than two years after its creation, Governor Martin quietly allowed the Western North Carolina Environmental Council to go out of business rather than sign an executive order extending its life. Sources close to the Governor said he was unhappy with the lack of achievement by the Council and was especially displeased with Gardner's lackluster performance as chairman.

The Drug Cabinet is essentially a paper entity. Its mission is to implement a plan of action to make North Carolina drug free. Many specialists in human behavior and substance abuse agree that making North Carolina drug free is unrealistic, unreasonable and most certainly beyond the ability of mortals to achieve. This "mission impossible" ironically, seems suited to Gardner's record of promising more than can be delivered.

To achieve a drug-free society would entail draconian regulation on many areas of the medical profession as well as the elimination of many products which are considered legal, but which contribute to the drug problem in the nation and the state.

The harsh truth about the drug problem is that there are no easy answers, no simple solutions, no political action that has worked in the past or shows much promise of solving the problem in the future.

Charles Dunn, Director of the North Carolina State Bureau of Investigation reports that there are 750,000 adults and 62,000 children in the Tar Heel state suffering from substance abuse problems.

In addition, reports Dunn, there are 84,000 adults and 40,000 children with severe mental illness--some of which may be the consequence of substance abuse--and 117,000 people with developmental disabilities. Altogether, reports Dunn, there are over 900,000 North Carolinians who need individual support and treatment--one at a time--from a "system that is inadequate and probably broken down."

Dunn estimates that it will cost the state at least $600 million to provide necessary programs and services in the next five years.

North Carolina's drug, alcohol and crime problems will not go away "by passing more laws and building more prisons. Too often, says Dunn, "alcoholics and drug addicts can't get help and treatment and they end up in the streets--and then in trouble with the law.

"*In most counties today,*" says Dunn, "*the jail is the largest mental health facility, but it offers no special care and treatment for the mentally ill or for substance abusers. If these people could be diverted to treatment facilities, they would have hope of being helped and jails and prisons would have space for criminals.*"

As chairman of the Drug Cabinet, Gardner cast the drug problem as an "us against them" struggle. He seemed unable or unwilling to acknowledge that the drug problem requires that we recognize that everyone plays a role in the creation of the problem and that a profound attitude change must occur throughout society if the problem is to be dealt with in a positive and productive manner.

As chairman of the Drug Cabinet, much of what Gardner said and did seemed to be designed to focus favorable attention on himself rather than to affect the drug problem in a substantive way.

One program in which a restaurant chain paid for signs to be posted on school grounds that included the words "Drug Free Zone" along with the name of the restaurant has drawn editorial criticism from major newspapers. Gardner also posted large billboard signs along highways that promoted the Drug Cabinet, and he has posed for pictures in drug-ravaged neighborhoods and in hospitals with babies damaged by cocaine.

One of the ideas advanced by Gardner and the Drug Cabinet was a "Marijuana Watch" in which landowners and others across the state would keep an eye out for marijuana plants that might have been planted by drug dealers on property which they did not own.

After 18 months, Gardner called a news conference to announce the fruits of the project. When newsman assembled, he displayed 22 puny marijuana plants which a state employee had found growing on the right-of-way of I-95 near Benson.

After 18 months and the expenditure of nearly $123,000 on the project, Gardner was able to show off 22 small marijuana plants that could have been growing wild.

The cost of each plant destroyed under Gardner's "Marijuana Watch" program was $5,590.

As chairman of the North Carolina Drug Cabinet, Gardner presided over a political activity that he has hoped would inure to his advantage as a candidate for Governor.

He can point to no personal activity or achievement that represents lasting success in persuading people not to use or traffic in drugs.

Not a single drug-related bill sponsored by Gardner and the Drug Cabinet has ever been enacted. Even members of the Republican administration, as well as members of the Drug Cabinet have publicly criticized the plan to make North Carolina drug free as being unsound. Dr. Jonnie McLeod, chairperson of the Governor's Council on Alcohol and Drug Abuse Among Children and Youth believes the plan to make North Carolina drug free indicates a "serious lack of understanding of the disease of addiction."

During his first year in office as chairman of the Drug Cabinet, Gardner appointed Paul Richardson, the manager of his 1988 campaign for Lieutenant Governor, as the Executive Director of the Cabinet at an annual fee of $57,477. All of the other members appointed by Gardner had been large Gardner campaign contributors.

Richardson left the post of Executive Director after a year, and was succeeded by Don Beason, who worked from April, 1990, to October, 1991, when he was succeeded by Janet Pueschel.

Although Pueschel had served under both previous executive directors before being named to the chief administrative position, she professed to know nothing of the Cabinet's finances.

"I have no idea how much our budget is and how it is spent," she said as recently as May 9, 1992. *"You'll have to ask someone else, probably the crime commission."*

During the time that Pueschel served under Executive Director Richardson, the Drug Cabinet budget was $426,130. Of that budget, $332,913 was paid in salaries to Gardner's former political supporters.

Asked to name the major contribution of the Drug Cabinet in dealing with the drug problem in North Carolina, Pueschel exclaimed in a tone of exasperation, *"The Drug Cabinet doesn't do anything!"*

The *"1991 Achievement Report to Governor James G. Martin"* published by the Drug Cabinet bears out Pueschel's statement. The report describes the work of a number of state offices, divisions and departments which have been active in drug problems for a number of years. The report disclosed no area in which progress has been made in dealing with the drug problem in North Carolina which was initiated or implemented by the so-called Drug Cabinet.

The 1991 report does, however, mention Gardner, and/or the office of Lieutenant Governor some 50 times in 25 pages.

Gardner has been highly critical of North Carolina's judicial system for what he termed "the coddling of criminals." He was so far off base that James Exum, Chief Justice of the North Carolina Supreme Court, was moved to issue a rare public statement exposing Gardner's ignorance.

North Carolina judges historically impose some of the nation's harsher sentences, said Justice Exum. Exum pointed out that it was the paroles board of the Republican administration, of which Gardner was a member, that turned drug dealers and other criminals out on the streets after serving a fraction of their initial sentences.

Since he announced his intentions to seek the office of Governor, Gardner has made a number of proposals which he contends will solve most of North Carolina's problems.

His proposals for education are to reduce what he terms the "bureaucracy in Raleigh" and provide what he calls "block grant funds to the local level without strings attached." He says he is in favor of reducing classroom size in grades K-3 to 15 students, and he is in favor of increasing teacher salaries.

Gardner says he can improve public education without raising taxes simply by cutting the "bureaucracy." He stated that belief in 1991 when the General Assembly was wrestling with the huge budget deficits.

Rep. Harry Payne, the co-chairman of the House Appropriations Subcommittee on Education, pointed out that "you could fire everyone in the education building and achieve savings of only one fourth the amount needed."

Payne, who won the Democratic nomination for Labor Commissioner in 1992, added that "you could fire everyone down to the principal's office and still not save enough money to do what Gardner proposed."

Gardner has not put a price tag on his proposal to reduce class size in grades K-3 to only 15 pupils but the cost has been estimated by some experts as high as $1.2 billion. To achieve sufficient savings through reductions in state government could play havoc with the state's economy as well as its ability to carry out laws and enforce regulations.

In a number of counties, the state of North Carolina is a major employer. In the counties of the Research Triangle which fuel the engine of the economy in perhaps a dozen surrounding counties, state government plays a crucial role in the stability of the economy.

To reduce state government by as much as Gardner contends is possible, says State Treasurer Harlan Boyles, could result in serious economic dislocation. *"Gardner's proposed reduction would mean the loss of perhaps 50,000 jobs statewide-- the equivalent of closing down the entire Research Triangle Park,"* says Boyles. *"To lose such a significant part of the employment base would have very serious and long term consequences on the economy of the state. To be sure, we need to reduce state government but not in such a manner that would create chaos and great misery for the people we must serve."*

Boyles added, *"Jim Gardner needs to be specific in how he would propose to re-allocate state funds, and which programs he would reduce or eliminate. Talking in such broad generalities cannot be taken seriously, but rather sounds like political rhetoric."*

Gardner has specifically identified only one example of the kind of government extravagance which he says could be reduced-- the $32 million new education building in Raleigh. He has criticized the building as a wasteful, plush facility for bureaucrats. Strangely he has been quiet about construction of the new revenue building next door to the education building, which was recommended by the Martin Administration. The cost of the revenue building is approximately the same as that of the education building. By contemporary standards, neither building is plush and their lobbies, offices, and amenities are pretty standard for new state government buildings.

Whether the education building was essential to the functioning of state government is a topic of legitimate debate. However, the need for the building was debated -- by appropriate elected officials who deemed the structure to be necessary and its cost reasonable. To dispute the need after the debate has been resolved and the building completed seems to serve no useful purpose.

Gardner advocates changing the state's budget procedure so as to base an upcoming year's budget on the revenues collected during the previous year. He favors the construction of more prisons, with prison inmates building their own cells.

He wants to stimulate home buying by giving first-time home buyers tax credits, and he is in favor of granting tax benefits to lending institutions which lend money to businesses that are going to use the money for the purchase of equipment to be used in North Carolina.

To control health care costs, Gardner proposes limiting the rights of patients to collect damages for injuries they might suffer as a result of malpractice by physicians and hospitals.

the second "businessman" governor elected in the 20th Century. The other businessman to hold the post was Luther Hodges. A comparison of the two men might be the best way to determine the kind of Governor Gardner might be.

Luther Hodges was born the son of a poor tenant farmer, and from those humble beginnings became a highly successful businessman, Lieutenant Governor, and Governor who brought into reality North Carolina's Research Triangle. Hodges led a program of industrial development that resulted in a new business locating in North Carolina or an existing one expanding every day of his administration. Hodges also served as Secretary of the U. S. Department of Commerce.

Jim Gardner was born the son of a wealthy family, and by the time he reached middle age he had lost everything in a string of business failures and today owns not even the house in which he and his family live.

A Distinguished Professorship in Business Ethics at the University of North Carolina was established in honor of Hodges.

Gardner's business career could easily become a textbook example of poor business practices.

Gardner's business and political record clearly does not qualify him to lead North Carolina. Without question, there are men and women more qualified than Gardner to lead the Republican Party in North Carolina.

Why then have Republicans nominated for the Office of Governor a man with a record so checkered that it casts profound doubts on his character?

The answer may reside with Jack Hawke, chairman of the North Carolina Republican Party.

Hawke and Gardner have been friends and associates for 30 years, politically joined at the hip. Many people believe Hawke was the architect of Gardner's political success in 1966 as well as the midwife at his rebirth as a socially acceptable political candidate in 1988.

Hawke sees 1992 as a pivotal time in his campaign to bring a lasting two-party system to North Carolina.

"*Both parties have a great stake in the outcome of the Governor's race in 1992,*" says Hawke. "*Martin has not been very partisan. Gardner as Governor would be a better asset for the party in that he would work through the party more and make building the Republican Party stronger a higher priority.*

"Moreover," says Hawke, *"The Democrats are afraid of him,"*

Long-time Democrats as well as mainline Republicans scoff at Hawke's assertions about Gardner's interest in party-building.

"Gardner is the last Republican horse Hawke has to ride," said one.

Since reentering politics in 1988, Gardner has sought to present his failures in business and politics in sanitized euphemisms. He calls them "setbacks" and "reversals", terms that deliberately obscure the stark reality of his bad timing, his poor judgment and his lack of management skills.

It is his attempts to redefine his record as well as his response to the events that constitute his record that leave in question the character of Jim Gardner.

XII

Unanswered Questions

Both journalism and history are enriched by the cooperation of persons about whom news articles and history are written. For that reason, conscientious journalists and careful historians sometimes go to extraordinary lengths to solicit the views of the participants in or eyewitnesses to newsworthy and historical events.

In the interest of good reporting, editorial balance and political credibility, we sought to interview Gardner about the significant events of his life and times. We called his various offices and we discussed our interests with Gardner's staff members and his political handlers.

We wrote letters, submitted questions in writing, made commitments to Gardner's political campaign manager to discuss matters which might reflect poorly upon Gardner in a manner that would provide ample opportunity for Gardner's views to be presented--properly in context.

Our efforts came to nought. Gardner would not discuss any of the issues concerning his business or political record.

Indeed, he would not answer even the most basic questions concerning himself.

Gardner partisans might well question why the authors chose to write a book about Gardner. It is a fair question. The answer is that Gardner asks voters to entrust the leadership of North Carolina to him on the basis of his record in business and politics. That record is flawed. Gardner's performance as a U.S. Congressman is nothing less than shameful. His performance as a candidate in five different campaigns indicates a strong propensity for manipulating the truth to his own ends. His record in business is a record of failure after failure.

Political memory is fleeting. More than half the voters who will decide the 1992 election were children when Gardner first entered the political scene in 1964. Quite a few were not born. Many who might have remembered the early days of Jim Gardner are dead.

A book that comprehensively and accurately lays out the record of a public figure with a past such as Gardner's who asks for the trust of the people seems not only desirable but decidedly necessary.

This book was not written to hurt Gardner and his supporters or to please his opponents and their supporters. It was written to serve the public. It contains more information than any single newspaper will present on a major candidate and, certainly, more than any broadcast station will provide.

In writing this book, we have made every attempt to cite our sources and to include a comprehensive bibliography. Many people who know Gardner, his family and his associates were anxious to tell us about this charismatic and enigmatic man. Many wanted to tell us about Gardner without disclosing their own identity. In most cases we have cited the source of information provided by individuals. In four instances, we complied with requests for anonymity because the requests were based not on political but personal considerations.

We are disappointed that Gardner would not discuss various aspects of his life with us. Certainly, he had no obligation to accommodate us. However, we feel he does owe the public answers to questions that have remained unanswered for decades.

In keeping with our promise to his campaign manager,

Steve Hooks, we provided Gardner with a list of questions raised in this book and gave him ample opportunity to answer them. He chose not to respond.

We are confident that the questions we posed to Gardner deserve answers. Since he did not answer them, we leave the questions with you, the reader.

1. You contend that your business experience qualifies you to be Governor and that you would run North Carolina Government on a business-like basis. Except for Hardee's, which grew into an international business following your departure, all of your business ventures failed. Please comment on this contradiction and indicate why you feel your business record qualifies you to be governor.

2. Our inquiry indicates that your business activities resulted in dozens of legal judgments being lodged against you in various courts and that the majority of them have not been satisfied. How many judgments have been filed against you; how many have you paid; and what are the dollar amounts of judgments you have paid as well as those you have not paid?

3. In federal court Hardee's was successfully sued in the mid-60s for the misuse of advertising materials. Your advertising agent, Gene Lewis, testified that he had urged you not to use the materials in question, but that you demanded they be used without authorization. Please give us your view of this episode.

4. Your property tax statement from Nash County shows that you currently own no real or personal property. Moreover, we can find no record of your owning and paying taxes on property in any North Carolina county. Do you own any property in North Carolina on which you pay property taxes? If so, where is the property, what is its value and how much in taxes do you pay?

5. If elected, you would be the first Governor of North Carolina in the 20th Century without a college degree. Please describe your intellectual and/or scholarly achievements that would offset this lack of academic credentials.

6. You were indicted by a grand jury for securities violations in connection with the Family Inns of America business which failed. Please provide your perspective on this incident.

7. A Durham newspaper reported that your businesses had defaulted on at least $34 million in loans and left $2.7 million in unpaid bills to some 450 suppliers and employees. Is this accurate? If not, please comment. If it is accurate, please provide your perspective.

8. As a congressman, you compiled a record of absences from your duties that placed you among the small group of congressmen with the worst attendance records in history. What were the reasons for your absences?

9. During 1968, you missed every meeting of the House Committee on Education and Labor, and the year before, missed half of the meetings. Please explain these absences during a time when our public school system was undergoing wrenching changes?

10. In your campaign for Governor in 1968, you indicated on a number of occasions that you could support George Wallace as easily as you could support Richard Nixon. Why did you feel this way then, and do you still think Wallace would have been as good a President as Nixon?

11. Mainstream Republicans in 1968, including Congressman Charles Jonas, known as "Mr. Republican" in North Carolina, were highly critical of your support of Wallace. They felt your position was detrimental to the growth of the Republican Party in North Carolina. Do you now feel that you were not a party loyalist, or do you think your critics were wrong? Please provide a comprehensive perspective.

12. Following the 1968 Primary, when Reginald Hawkins, the black candidate for the Democratic nomination for Governor, announced his support for Bob Scott, you charged that Scott had made some kind of sinister deal with Hawkins to advance the agenda of black people. The Charlotte Observer said you lied.

Did you have evidence of some kind of unethical deal between Scott and Hawkins? If so, what did you know?

13. In the 1972 Republican Primary, Jim Holshouser requested you debate him a number of times but you refused. Yet, in the second primary, you repeatedly demanded that Holshouser engage in a debate with you. Please provide your perspective on the reasons for your change in attitude regarding debates.

14. According to published reports following your defeat by Gov. Holshouser, you were less than gracious. Are you proud of the way you behaved following the second 1972 Republican Primary? Please provide your perspective.

15. Following the first primary in 1972, you called a news conference to announce that the White House had asked Holshouser to withdraw from the campaign because it felt he could not win and would hurt Nixon's candidacy against McGovern. Harry Dent, Presidential Aide from South Carolina, came to Charlotte and said you had told a falsehood. Please comment on this incident and, if you can, provide the name of the person in the White House who said that Governor Holshouser should withdraw.

16. Ms. Janet Pueschel, Executive Director of the NC Drug Cabinet told us that the "Drug Cabinet doesn't do anything." Please provide your perspective on the contributions of the Drug Cabinet in dealing with what you have termed North Carolina's most serious social problem.

17. You have been quoted in published reports as saying you were not aware of the seriousness of the drug problem in North Carolina in 1988 when you campaigned for Lieutenant Governor. Many people, who have been troubled by this terrible problem for nearly 20 years, find that statement astounding. First, were you quoted correctly, and if so, please expound on your position; and second, if you were not quoted correctly, please provide your correct position.

18. You frequently mention that you co-founded Hardee's. Wilber

Hardee said he founded the first Hardee's Restaurant after which you and Leonard Rawls tricked him out of his business and his name. Please give your version of how Hardee's was established.

19. You also say from time to time that you once headed Hardee's. However, company records today indicate that you never held any office higher than vice president. Please explain the difference in these stories.

20. Why did you not rejoin Hardee's in 1968?

21. Do you believe David Wilson filed suit against you in the Family Inns of America matter for any reason other than to get his money back?

22. You have been quoted in published reports recently saying you have never declared bankruptcy, yet you participated in the filing for bankruptcy protection of the Modular Corporation of America as vice president of the company. Please explain your thoughts on this apparent contradiction.

23. Peter Ploss, an associate at Carolando, was quoted in a Durham newspaper calling you a "snake-oil salesman," and has said you are "perhaps the world's greatest salesman but its worst manager." Please explain why you may disagree.

24. In the Virginia Waffle Shoppes venture you were associated with Joe Palumbo who was identified by testimony in the US House Banking Committee as having ties through a relative to organized crime. During your business dealings with Mr. Palumbo were you aware of his ties to organized crime?

25. Testimony in the House Banking Committee also revealed that you had filed for a SBA loan on behalf of the Virginia Waffle Shoppes as a "minority" entrepreneur. Please give your recollection of this incident.

26. You were sued by Parker's Barbecue in 1982 for breach of contract and for attempting to mis-appropriate their good name.

Please give your version of this matter.

27. You were also sued by TGI Friday's for infringing on their good name with your Friday's 1890 Seafood Restaurants. Please give your version of this matter.

28. Although Tony Rand will not say so specifically, his demeanor when talking about the libel suit he brought against you indicates strongly that you paid him handsomely to drop the case. Did you or your insurance company pay Tony Rand to drop the suit. If so, how much?

29. The full page ad in the May 30, 1992, issue of the <u>News and Observer</u> said you had several business successes since Hardee's. Please list them.

30. What is your business philosophy?

Following is the text of a letter submitted to Governor Jim Martin, through his press secretary on May 22, 1992. The Governor did not respond.

"Grady Jefferys and I are writing a book about Lieutenant Governor Jim Gardner. Would you get for us, a brief statement from Governor Martin about the Lieutenant Governor. We would like for Governor Martin to identify the achievements of Mr. Gardner, as a key member of the Martin Administration during the past three and one-half years, as well as Mr. Gardner's special strength of character and the overall political vision which he feels qualifies the Lieutenant Governor to succeed him as Governor of North Carolina."

Bibliography

Chapter 1
North Carolina Governors, 1585-1975, North Carolina Division of Archives and History; Corporate brochure published by Hardee's Food Systems, Inc., and Last Will and Testament of Arthur Lynwood Tyler, Nash County Courthouse records.

Chapter 2
1. Hardees--Interviews with Wilber Hardee, Fall of 1991. Annual Report, promotional literature, Hardees Food Systems. Court Documents, Phil Davis Musical vs. Hardees Food System, US Records Center, Atlanta, GA. Court documents, Nash County Courthouse, Nashville, NC.
2. Family Inns of America--Court Documents, US District Court of Eastern NC, Wilson, Raleigh: David S. Wilson vs. James C. Gardner, et al (74-59-C): Court documents, NC Superior Court, Wilmington, NC, State of NC vs. James C. Gardner (76-CR-5350-57); Court Documents, Biggs, Meadows, Batts, Etheridge & Winberry vs. James C. Gardner, Nash County Courthouse (77-CVD-615, Book 19, Page 48).
3. Modular Corporation of America--Court Documents, US District Court for the Western District of NC, Charlotte Division, In the Matter of: Modular Corporation of America, Bankrupt. (C. B. 74-63), Calvin W. Chesson, as Trustee in Modular Corporation of America Bankruptcy v. James and Marie Gardner, Charlotte, NC 1976.
4. Carolando--Press Release issued by Jim Gardner in 1972. Various news reports.
5. Brandywine Bay--Court Documents, Carteret County, 1975 Foreclosure on Brandywine Bay by Cameron Brown Financial Investment Group.
6. Virginia Waffle Shoppes-- Hearings by the U.S. House of Representatives Subcommittee on Minority Small Business Enterprise and Franchising, Washington, D. C. October 3, 4, 1973; Hearings before the Subcommittee on Small Business of the Committee on Banking and Currency, November 27-30, December 4, 10, 11, 1973. The SBA Investigation Report, April 9, 1974.
7. Parker's Barbecue--Court Documents NC Superior Court,

Wilson, NC; Parker's Franchise System, Inc, Plaintiff vs. James Carson Gardner, John G. Gardner, and Gardner Foods, Inc., Defendants (82-CVS-577).

8. Court Documents US District Court, Eastern District of NC, Raleigh; Norma Jean Burnley and David A. Hendricks, Plaintiffs, vs. Gardner Foods, Inc, Defendant (87-521-CIV-5)

9. Court documents, Wake County Superior Court: Salpeg Corporation vs. Gardner's Barbecue of Westridge, Inc., and James C. Gardner, a complaint.

Chapter 3

"The Congressional Papers of James C. Gardner", North Carolina Collection, University of North Carolina, Chapel Hill, NC; The Presidential Character, Prentice-Hall, Inc., The Oxford Companion To the Mind, Oxford University Press.

Chapter 4

Interviews with Wilber Hardee, Fall of 1991. Annual Report, promotional literature, Hardees Food Systems. Court Documents, Phil Davis Musical vs. Hardees Food System, US Records Center, Atlanta, Ga. Court Documents, Nash County Courthouse.

Chapter 5

Associated Press Features; Various North Carolina newspapers; Gardner campaign advertisement; Politics Battle Plan, The McMillan Company, Inc.; Chain Reaction, The Impact of Race, Rights and Taxes on American Politics, W. W. Norton & Company; Dan Moore campaign materials, prepared by J. T. Howard Advertising Agency, Inc.

Chapter 6

The Congressional Papers of James C. Gardner, 23 boxes, NC Collection, University of North Carolina at Chapel Hill.

Chapter 7

Various North Carolina newspapers; author's notes from Broughton campaign for Governor, Associated Press reports; Chain Reaction, the Impact of Race, Rights and Taxes on American Politics.

Chapter 8

Court Documents: US District Court of Eastern NC, Wilson, Raleigh; David S. Wilson vs. James C. Gardner, et al (74-59-C); NC Superior Court, Wilmington, NC; State of NC vs. James C. Gardner (76-CR-5350-57); Nash County Courthouse, Nashville,

NC, Biggs, Meadows, Batts, Etheridge & Winberry vs. James C. Gardner (77-CVD-615).

Chapter 9

Depositions by Herman Gaskins and Jim Gardner to H. Gerald Beaver and Harold E. Carlin, attorneys at law.

Chapter 10

Same as for Chapter 2

Chapter 11

Gardner campaign materials; interview with Jack Hawke; interview with Harlan Boyles, Treasurer of North Carolina; Various North Carolina newspapers.

ABOUT THE AUTHORS:

Grady Jefferys, a newspaper, magazine and television writer for more than 30 years, has written extensively on North Carolina topics and has participated at a professional level in many political campaigns in the Tar Heel State. He is the author and/or co-author of five other books.

Charles Heatherly, a 1964 graduate of the University of North Carolina at Chapel Hill, with a degree in journalism, covered Jim Gardner's 1966 campaign for Congress and has been an ardent student of North Carolina politics for the past quarter century.